MEMOIRS

OF THE

LIFE AND WRITINGS

OF

VITTORIO ALFIERI.

"ALFIERI IS THE GREAT NAME OF THIS AGE."
LORD BYRON.

LONDON:

CHARLES AND HENRY BALDWYN. NEWGATE-STREET.

1821.

Vittorio Alfieri.

Published by C. & H. Baldwyn, Newgate Street.

ADVERTISEMENT.

It was at first the intention of the writer of this SKETCH
to have presented the public with a translation of Al-
fieri's own MEMOIRS OF HIS LIFE, *and to have sup-*
plied additional facts and explanatory observations in
the notes. A careful re-perusal of the original nar-
rative convinced him, that a much smaller work might
be made to embrace every topic of interest or informa-
tion in the Life of Alfieri. There is a strong and a
natural prejudice in favour of auto-biography; but
the narrative in question possesses none of the graces
and interest peculiar to that species of composition. It
has none of the passionate earnestness of Rousseau, or
of the vivacious garrulity of Marmontel and Goldoni;

it is a dry, unimpressive detail of facts and opinions, neither enlivened by anecdote or ennobled by feeling. The Author never descends from his tragic elevation, to converse on equal terms with the reader : he registers the follies of his youth and the passions of his manhood with stoical coldness and patrician dignity. The strict veracity of Alfieri has never been called in question, but his personal and political feelings give a colouring to his narration, at once fallacious and repulsive. It is presumed, that the present publication will be found to possess all the information, without the diffuseness of the original work, and to comprise, in a readable form, every incident and trait in the life and character of Alfieri, which can assist the English Reader in forming a correct estimate of the talents and eccentricities of the greatest of Italian Dramatists.

MEMOIRS OF ALFIERI.

CHAPTER THE FIRST. 1749-1758.

Infancy.

VITTORIO ALFIERI was born on the 17th of
January, 1749, at Asti, in Piedmont, of noble
and wealthy parents. His father, Antonio Alfieri,
was a man of strict morals and great simplicity
of manners. After remaining unmarried until
upwards of fifty, he became enamoured of the
young widow of the Marquis of Cacherano, a
nobleman of Asti. The fruit of this union was
a daughter; and, two years after, a son, whose
birth was a source of infinite joy to his father,
who was anxious to have his name perpetuated.
The young Vittorio was sent to nurse in the
village of Rovigliasco, two miles from Asti,

B

where his father, who was still hearty and robust, came to see him almost every day, in defiance of the weather. In one of these excursions he over-heated himself, and was attacked by an inflammation in his lungs, which in a few days carried him off. His widow was left pregnant with another boy, who died in his infancy; and, besides her children by Alfieri, had two daughters and a son, by her first husband, living. She was still young and handsome, and espoused for her third husband the Chevalier Hyacinth de Magliano, the representative of a different branch of the Alfieri family, who had succeeded to an immense property by the death of his elder brother. Vittorio and his sister Julia experienced the utmost kindness from their new parent.

The signora's eldest son and daughter were successively sent to Turin; the one to the College of Jesuits, the other to a convent. Shortly after, Julia was placed in a convent at Asti, to the great grief of Vittorio, between whom and his sister the strongest affection existed. A

worthy priest, named Ivaldi, was taken into the
family as the preceptor of Vittorio, now in his
seventh year, from.whom he learned writing and
the first rules of arithmetic : Ivaldi, also, taught
him to read Cornelius Nepos and Phædrus's
Fables ; but, being himself extremely illiterate,
the education of his pupil, while under his care,
was confined to these moderate acquirements.
His parents had no taste for, or knowledge of
literature, and were unable to discern and remedy the incompetence of his preceptor. Vittorio had naturally a turn for study ; and the
solitude in which he lived with his tutor, gene-
rated a habit of melancholy and abstraction,
deepened and embittered by his separation from
his beloved sister. His visits to her, which had,
at first, been daily, were made less and less frequent, that he might bestow undivided attention on his important studies. The greatest
pleasure he experienced at this period of his
life, was in frequenting a Carmelite Church, adjoining his paternal mansion. The music, the
ceremonies of high mass, the processions, and

other imposing spectacles of the Catholic ritual, made a deep impression on the ardent mind of Vittorio. The youthful and innocent countenances of the Carmelite novices, who assisted at the different festivals, in the white robes of their order, inspired him with veneration and love. Their features and gestures were unceasingly present to his imagination, and his childish enthusiasm arrayed them with the beauty and attributes of heavenly beings. These contemplations rather increased than alleviated that habitual melancholy, which, even at this early period, began to prey on the mind of Alfieri. His studies were neglected; employment and society were alike irksome to him:—and the juvenile recluse, with a precocity of desperation unexampled in the annals of suicide, made a serious attempt to free himself from the burthen of existence. In one of his melancholy fits, recollecting that hemlock was destructive of life, he devoured by handfuls such weeds as he could find, in hopes that the deadly plant might be amongst them. The sickness which followed

this exploit discovered the project of the desperate boy, and proper medicines being administered, he escaped without any other punishment than a few days' confinement to his
chamber. Alternately taciturn and petulant,
reserved and talkative, his spirits fluctuated
from one extreme to the other. Dreading a
reprimand, he was insensible to any other method of 'restraint; timid, but inflexible, when
coercion was attempted. The punishment which
most bitterly afflicted Vittorio, was the being
sent to mass with a net on his head, in the
shape of a night-cap, which almost concealed
his hair; and, on one occasion, his horror at
being exposed in this equipment, made him violently ill for some days, and saved him from any
future infliction of the same kind.

When 'scarcely eight years of age, he was
ordered to make his *confession* to a priest, and
his worthy preceptor, Ivaldi, prepared him for
the ceremony, by suggesting all the crimes of
which he conceived his pupil might have been
guilty, though he was scarcely acquainted with

their names. On the appointed day he prostrated himself at the feet of Father Ange, his mother's confessor, but pride and obstinacy kept him silent. The holy Father, however, declared himself satisfied, and granted absolution to the impenitent youth, enjoining him, as a penance, to throw himself at his mother's feet, before sitting down to dinner, and publicly to solicit pardon for his past offences. Vittorio felt no repugnance to asking pardon of his mother, but his proud spirit could not submit to kneel before those who might happen to be present. On his return, he found a large party assembled in the dining-room, and advanced irresolutely to seat himself with the others. His mother, who had concerted his penance with the Confessor, with a stern look, asked him, if he had a right to place himself at the table; if he had fulfilled his duty, and had nothing to reproach himself with? Though overcome with confusion and grief, Vittorio remained obstinately silent; and there being no way of enforcing his penance, without discovering the juggling of the Confessor, he escaped with the loss of his dinner, and was enjoined no public penance in future.

His half-brother, the Marquis of Cacherano, who had been for some time past receiving his education at Turin, came to pass the vacation at Asti, in the summer of 1757. He had seen something of the world, and could construe Virgil; and his superior knowledge, as well as the possession of money and freedom from controul, impressed the mind of Vittorio with a painful sense of inferiority, which prevented any cordial friendship from existing between them. The company of the Marquis, however, made the time pass more pleasantly than it had hitherto done. In one of their sports, while the Marquis was teaching Vittorio the Prussian exercise, the latter, in making a quick turn, fell down, and his head coming in contact with the andiron, he received a severe wound. When sufficiently recovered to go abroad, Vittorio felt proud of his bandages; and when his Tutor, in reply to any inquiries, answered, that he had had a fall, the young hero took care to add, *in performing my exercise.*

In the following year his paternal uncle, the Chevalier Pellegrino Alfieri, to whom the care of his fortune had been confided, returning from his travels in France, Holland, and England, arrived at Asti. Finding his nephew's education had been entirely neglected, he determined on placing him in the Academy at Turin, to the great grief of his mother, who had recently lost her eldest son, the Marquis, by a pulmonary complaint. Vittorio, who had hardly ever been a dozen miles from home, was delighted with the prospect before him; but when the day of parting arrived, his courage failed him, and he was placed almost by force in the carriage. The rapidity of their journey, and the succession of new and striking objects, soon dispelled his regrets, and he entered Turin with rapturous anticipations. After remaining a short time at the house of his uncle, to the great annoyance of the latter, he was placed in the Academy, and abandoned, in his tenth year, in a great measure to his own discretion, or rather to his fortune. He was attended by a domestic, named André, a young man of good natural parts, who had received a better education than the generality of his rank in life, but who took advantage of his young master's unprotected situation, to neglect and ill treat him.

CHAPTER THE SECOND.   1758-1763.

His Academical Education.

THE Academy was a spacious quadrangular building, with a large court in the middle. Two sides of the quadrangle were occupied by the students; the other sides were formed by the Theatre Royal and the Royal Archives. That part of the building which was allotted to the students, was divided into the *first, second,* and *third apartments.* The *third apartment,* to which Alfieri belonged, was devoted to the juvenile academicians: the *second,* to adults: the *first* was almost solely occupied by foreigners, (of whom a great proportion were English, Russians, and Germans), and by the Pages of the King, whose gay and idle life afforded no very edifying example to the other inmates. The foreigners,

too, by their extravagance and freedom from
controul, excited the envy and dislike of the rest
of the students. The Professors took no care to
form the minds and morals of their pupils; and
while. they complied, in appearance, with the
regulations of the Academy, which were partial,
arbitrary, and inefficient, exercised no further
attention towards them. In the Academy, Vittorio improved his Latin rather by the force
of emulation than from the instructions of his
tutor, a priest, who possessed all the ignorance
of Ivaldi, without his kindness and attention.
The scholars learned to translate the lives of
Cornelius Nepos; but none of them, nor even
their masters, knew any thing of the individuals
commemorated. At the end of the first year of
his abode at the Academy, a copy of Ariosto's
Orlando Furioso fell in his way, which he purchased of one of his fellow-students, volume by
volume, in exchange for the half of the chicken
which each scholar was allowed for his Sunday's
dinner. This work he perused unceasingly,
though he understood it very imperfectly. So

much had the most important part of his education been neglected, that, though he could
translate Virgil's *Georgics*, he was unable to
comprehend the most easy of Italian poets. His
secret studies were, however, soon put an end
to, by his Ariosto being discovered, and taken
from him by the Sub-Prior.

At the end of two years, Alfieri was little
improved in learning, and much deteriorated in
health. The scanty and bad diet, and the ab-
surdly short time allowed the students for sleep,
checked his growth, and rendered him sickly
and emaciated. He was afflicted with an erup-
tive disorder, resembling leprosy; his body was
covered with ulcers, and he became the sport of
his companions, who bestowed on him signifi-
cant and opprobrious nicknames.

His uncle had been appointed Governor of
Coni, where he resided eight months in the year.
The only relative who took any notice of Vittorio, was a cousin of his father's, Count Benedict Alfieri, who resided at Turin, and whom he
visited as often as his capricious valet would

permit. Count Benedict was first architect to
the King, and of great skill and celebrity in his
profession, for which he entertained the most
enthusiastic reverence. He never pronounced
the name of Michael Angelo without bowing
his head, or taking off his hat, and frequently
expatiated to his youthful relative on the sublime genius of that great man. He always
treated Vittorio with much kindness, and the
latter was sincerely attached to him, in spite
of his fondness for architecture and Michael
Angelo.

Notwithstanding the incompetence and in-
attention of his preceptors, Alfieri, by the help
of a good memory, managed to get through his
tasks with some degree of credit, and was successively admitted into the rhetorical and philosophical classes. In consequence of this promo-
tion, he was removed into the *second apartment,*
the inmates of which were all older and stronger
than himself; but this circumstance rather increased than diminished his spirit and confidence, and served as a strong incentive to

exertion. He recovered his Ariosto by stealth
from the shelves of the Sub-Prior; but being
imperfectly acquainted with his language, and
bewildered in his labyrinth of tales, he laid
aside the book in despair. The *Æneid* of
Annibal Caro falling into his hands, he read it
more than once with great avidity. These two
works, with a few of the dramas of Metastasio
and Goldoni, constituted his whole stock of
Italian literature.

His uncle, the Governor, returned for a few
months to Turin, in the winter of 1762, and observing the bad health of Vittorio, obtained for.
him some indulgences in his diet and repose.
His sister Julia, whose education had been as
injudicious as his own, was now in her fifteenth
year. She had formed an attachment, of which
her uncle disapproved, though the object of it
was in every respect her equal, and he caused
her to be removed from the convent at Asti to
one at Turin. Her removal was a fortunate circumstance for her brother, who had now some
one to sympathise with his real or imaginary

griefs : he spent all the time of absence allowed him by the regulations of the Academy, in conversing or weeping with her at the grate, and her society tranquilized his mind, and sensibly ameliorated his health. His cousin, the Architect, took him during the vacation to the Theatre Carignanò, where he saw the opera-buffa of *Il Mercato di Malmantile*. The music, lively, impassioned, and diversified, made a deep and lasting impression on the mind of Alfieri. He felt himself overpowered by feelings, which he could neither define nor describe, and for several days remained in a profound, but not unpleasing, melancholy. The tumult and confusion of ideas which this emotion occasioned, produced a disrelish and incapacity for his studies, which he was a considerable time in overcoming.*

The first year of his studies in the philoso-

---

* In his riper years music continued to excite emotions in his mind approaching to inspiration. The plans of almost all his tragedies were conceived while listening to music, or soon after having heard it.

phical class being ended, his tutors took care to inform his uncle, that he had laboured with assiduity and success, and he was in consequence invited to pass some days with his relative at Coni. During his stay there he composed, or rather pilfered his first sonnet, from Ariosto and Metastasio: it was, as might be expected, lamentably deficient in rhyme and measure; for though he could string together Latin hexametres and pentametres, he was completely ignorant of the principles of Italian versification. This effusion was in praise of a lady, whom his uncle courted, and was infinitely admired by her, and by others who did not understand it. His uncle, unfortunately, was more attached to history and politics than to poetry, and so successfully ridiculed this juvenile composition, that Vittorio was effectually cured, for that time, of his poetical propensities.

The following year was spent in the study of natural and moral philosophy, under the celebrated Father Beccaria; but at the end of twelve months he was unable to retain a single defini-

tion in his head. This unprofitable study was
then exchanged for the canon and civil law—
a pursuit which, at the end of four years, exalts
the student to the height of academical glory—
a doctor's degree. After some weeks' application, he was afflicted with a return of his old
disorder, an eruption on the head, with increased
virulence. He was obliged to surrender his hair
to the hated scissars, and to assume a peruke,
which attracted the derision of all his fellow-
students, till he parried their jokes by being the
first to laugh at and maltreat the disagreeable
appendage. In the same year (1763) he had
masters assigned him in music and geography.
For the latter study he had a strong inclination,
especially when blended with history. Though
he felt a growing passion for music, he attained
little proficiency in the art, which he attributed
principally to his taking lessons immediately
after dinner. He made as little progress in the
use of arms and in dancing: for the first, his
bodily weakness almost disqualified him; and
for the latter, he always entertained an aversion,

which was increased by his dislike of his teacher,
a perfect Parisian *petit maître*, whose foppery
and polite impertinence first excited that anti-
pathy to the French character, which continued
through life a predominant feeling in the mind
of Alfieri. His geographical master lent him
occasionally some French books, and, among
others, *Gil Blas*, with which he was highly delighted. This was the first book he had read
from the beginning to the end, except the *Æneid*
of Annibal Caro. He read, besides, many romances, such as *Cassandra, Almachilde,* &c. but
the book which interested him beyond all others
was the *Memoires d'un Homme de Qualité,* of the
Abbé Prevôt.

During the summer of 1762, his uncle had
been appointed Viceroy of Sardinia, and, on
leaving Piedmont, had transferred the manage-
ment of Vittorio's pecuniary concerns to one of
his friends. This new guardian assigned him a
monthly stipend, which his uncle had always refused him, through the representations, he suspected, of his faithful André, who, for obvious

reasons, chose to have the control of his master's funds. This fellow had abandoned himself to drunkenness and debauchery, and treated Vittorio in the most insolent and brutal manner: when intoxicated, which frequently happened four or five times a week, he sometimes went so far as to beat him. During Vittorio's frequent illnesses, he would often go out and leave him locked up in his chamber from dinner to suppertime. The infamous conduct of this domestic tyrant was discovered by the new guardian, and he was immediately dismissed. His removal, however, greatly afflicted Vittorio, who had become from habit involuntarily attached to him. As André was forbidden to enter the Academy, he went to see him as often as he could get out, and gave him all his spare money. André at length got another situation, and time, and the change which took place in his circumstances, soon effaced from Vittorio's mind the remembrance of his unworthy domestic.

CHAPTER THE THIRD. 1763-1766.

He becomes his own Master.

AFTER six months' residence at Cagliari, the
Viceroy died; little regretted by his nephew,
to whom he had been a stern and severe, though
a faithful, guardian, His death put Vittorio in
possession of his father's property, increased by
a considerable legacy. The authority of the
guardian ceases in Piedmont at the age of fourteen, but the law appoints another guardian,
who, leaving to the minor the disposal of his
annual revenues, can only prevent him from
alienating his estates. The first and most valued advantage which Alfieri derived from the
death of his uncle was the privilege of attending
the Riding School, which had hitherto been denied him. The Prior of the Academy made his

attaining the rank of a Master of Arts the price
of this indulgence. Impelled by this stimulus,
he revived his recollections of logic, physics,
and geometry, and in fifteen or twenty days was
able to go through a negligent public examination : became, he hardly knew how, a Master of
Arts, and, what was of much more importance,
took his first lesson in horsemanship. Though
puny, sickly, and weak, his enthusiasm overcame every obstacle, and he soon became an ex-
pert horseman. Emancipated from the yoke of
his uncle, and of his valet—master of his property, and of a horse—he felt his pride and confidence daily increase. He boldly told the Prior
and his guardian that he was tired of the study
of the law, and was determined to pursue it no
longer ; and, finding him resolute, they removed
him to the *first apartment*, the inmates of which
were subject to no sort of restraint.

He took possession of his new quarters in
May, 1763, and remained there almost solitarily
during the summer, but with the winter arrived
a crowd of foreigners, principally English. A

well supplied table, abundance of amusement
and repose, little study, daily exercise on horseback, and, above all, the power of doing as he
pleased, speedily re-established his health and
vigour, and inspired him with spirit and vivacity.
His hair having grown afresh, he threw aside
his peruke, as well as the black habiliments
which he had been condemned, by the rules of
the Academy, to wear for the last five years,
and indulged his vanity in the most costly
dresses. Along with his liberty and fortune,
Alfieri acquired the usual accompaniments of
wealth—friends, companions, and parasites. He
did not, however, so completely abandon himself to pleasure as to forego his studies altogether. He felt uneasy and ashamed in reflecting
on the little progress he had made in the pursuit
of knowledge ; but having no friend whose taste
and judgement might direct him, and being
master of no language, he found himself at a
loss how and where to begin. The continued
perusal of French books, the society of foreigners, and the absence of opportunities of con-

versing in pure Italian, made him insensibly forget what little he had previously known of that language. With the French language he was so much more conversant, that in a fit of study, which lasted for two or three months, he attacked the thirty-six volumes of the *Histoire Ecclesiastique* of Fleuri, and read through nearly the whole of them, with great perseverance, and some degree of pleasure. Wearied, at length, with this dry and unprofitable study, he returned with increased avidity to his romances and *Les Milles et une Nuits.* Having contracted an intimacy with several young gentlemen of the city, they frequently sallied out on hired hacks, and performed abundance of pranks at the hazard of their necks; leaping over hedges and ditches, galloping down dangerous declivities, or fording the Doria at its confluence with the Po, and became so notorious for their temerity and excesses that no one would lend them horses on any terms.

Alfieri had no person who interfered with his pursuits except the new valet whom his guar-

diary had appointed, and who attended him
wherever he went. This fellow was docile and
good tempered, and was easily bribed into any
of his master's schemes ; but his continual attendance was a visible check which Alfieri could
not endure, and appeared to him peculiarly op-
pressive, as no other inmate of the *first apartment* was troubled with such a monitor. In reply to his remonstrances, his extreme youth was
objected, for he was not yet fifteen ; but, unsatisfied with this reason, he determined in future to
go out as he pleased, without consulting his valet or any other person. This conduct produced
a reprimand, and on his repetition of the offence, he was confined to his chamber. As soon
as he was set at liberty he went out as before,
and was visited with a confinement of increased
duration. He however continued obstinate, and
the punishment increasing with every repetition
of his offence, he was at last confined to his
chamber for three months together. During
this period he remained in bed the greater part
of the day, neglected his dress, and degenerated

in his appearance and manners into a mere savage. The marriage of his sister, Julia, with the Count Hyacinth de Cumiana put an end to his afflictions. His new brother-in-law obtained the remission of his punishment, and the same privileges which were enjoyed by his fellows. Alfieri accompanied the new-married couple to Cumiana, where he spent a month in gaiety and enjoyment, enhanced by his late privations. He had obtained an increased allowance from his guardian, and he now purchased a beautiful and spirited horse, of which he became dotingly fond. His passion for these animals increasing by indulgence, he purchased seven more horses in the course of the year. A spirit of rivalry between Alfieri and the academicians (particularly the English) led him into great expenses in his dress and manner of living. He had many acquaintances in the city, who, though of respectable families, were not in affluent circumstances, and he always felt reluctant to hurt their feelings by a display of superior profusion. After dining with his comrades in the academy, he would lay

c

aside his splendid dress, and assume a more
sober exterior, to visit his friends in the city.
After having purchased (in spite of the remonstrances of his guardian) an elegant carriage, he
never rode out in it, and contented himself with
riding on horseback; an exercise in which his
less wealthy friends could join him.

Going with two of his riding companions to
pass a month with them in the country, the
charms of their sister-in-law, a young and lively
brunette, made Alfieri feel, for the first time,
the passion of love. He became melancholy—
was embarrassed in her presence, and restless in
her absence. On his being separated from her
by the termination of his visit, he would waste
whole days in traversing the public walks, in
hopes of catching a glimpse of her. This passion never proceeded any farther; but for several years it haunted the imagination of Alfieri,
and acted as an incentive to distinction, in the
hope that, should circumstances change, he
might render himself worthy of her. In the
autumn of 1765, he accompanied his guardian

to Genoa; and, in his way to that city, revisited his mother and his native city for the first time since his separation from them. This excursion and the sight of the sea inspired him with an unconquerable desire for travelling, which he soon found an opportunity of indulging.

On entering the *first apartment*, he had inscribed his name among those who wished to serve in the army. Three years after, to his great mortification, his desire was complied with, and he reluctantly accepted a commission in the provincial regiment of Asti. This appointment obliged him to leave the academy, of which he had now been an inmate nearly eight years, and to which from habit he was sincerely attached. The regiment to which he belonged was called out only twice a year, for a few days; but Alfieri had too inveterate a dislike for military subordination to submit even to this transient duty with patience. After leaving the academy, Alfieri resided in the house of his sister, the Countess of Cumiana, and amused himself with squandering money in the purchase of horses, and the entertainment of his juvenile friends. Impatient to commence his intended travels, he embraced an opportunity which occurred of accompanying two young Dutchmen, who, with their preceptor, an English Catholic, were proceeding to Rome and Naples. He had to encounter and overcome the opposition of his brother-in-law, of his avaricious guardian, and of the king, (who did not encourage a taste for travelling among his nobility;) but his ardour and perseverance succeeded, and he set out on the 4th of October, 1766, on his much wished-for journey.

CHAPTER THE FOURTH. 1766-1767.

He commences his Travels.

HE was attended in this journey by a domestic
who had been in the service of his late uncle,
named Francis Elias. This person, who possessed a large share of acuteness and activity,·
had much more of the direction of the journey
than the young gentlemen or their preceptor.
He retained his authority in the subsequent
wanderings of Alfieri, who always placed the
most implicit confidence in his judgment and
integrity. The greatest pleasure which Alfieri
experienced in this excursion was from the rapidity with which they proceeded. They visited
Milan, Bologna, Placentia, Parma, Modena, Florence, Lucca, Pisa, Leghorn, and Sienna. The
only language which Alfieri spoke or wrote in

this excursion was French, and he could scarcely
think in any other. Even during their stay at Florence, he did not learn to appreciate the beauty
of the Tuscan dialect. Despising the people, he
had no wish to resemble them even in speech,
and began to study English under a very indifferent master, though he disliked the language as
much as he admired the national character. He
had, at this time, very little taste for sculpture,
and none for painting. For architecture, he had
an indistinct feeling of admiration, from its
being associated in his recollections with his
relative, Count Benedict, and the tomb of Michael Angelo called forth his warmest enthusiasm. The party, at length, proceeded to Rome,
which they reached in December. Alfieri felt
all the emotions natural to a young and ardent
mind, on beholding the former capital of the
world. The eight days which they passed in this
city were occupied in unremitting researches;
but the object which eclipsed every other in the
mind of Alfieri was St. Peter's, which he visited
twice every day during their residence at Rome.

On the approach of winter they proceeded to
Naples. In their way thither, Elias broke his
arm by a fall from his horse, but he contrived
to set it himself, and continued the journey
without appearing sensible of the pain of his
accident: the coolness and presence of mind
which he displayed on this occasion won his
master's esteem and admiration. The splendour
of Naples and the beauty of its scenery did not
compensate the juvenile travellers for the badness of the house and the gloominess of the
street in which they were obliged to lodge,
owing to the crowded state of the more conve-
nient hotels. Alfieri was introduced into society by the Sardinian ambassador, who presented him to the reigning King, Ferdinand IV.
then in his sixteenth year. The carnival was
much superior in gaiety and splendour to what
he had seen at Turin, and the fêtes and public
spectacles presented an unremitting succession
of amusements. But Alfieri was resolved not
to be pleased: master of himself and his actions
at eighteen—with an ample revenue and a pre-

possessing figure—he felt only satiety and disgust. His greatest pleasure was in attending
the opera-buffa, though its lively music rather
increased than alleviated his melancholy, and
in solitary rambles on the sea-shore. He had
made some acquaintances among the Neapolitan
gentry, but the natural reserve and hauteur of
his character precluded any intimate friendship
from existing between them. He felt all the
misery of living without an object or pursuit,
and hurried from place to place without wishing
to see any thing, and anxious only to escape
from the repose which was now insupportable to
him. During his stay at Naples, he began to
intrigue to, get rid of his travelling preceptor,
who, though easy and indulgent, was tedious
and irresolute. The Sardinian ambassador
wrote in his behalf to Turin, and gave so good
an account of his regularity and discretion, that
his request of emancipation was complied with.
The ambassador, pitying his irksome and unprofitable life, advised him to study politics, to
qualify him for a diplomatic career. Alfieri was

infinitely pleased with this idea, thinking a grave and sober exterior was all that was re-quired to constitute a statesman; but it pro-duced no other effect on him than to increase his natural taciturnity.

Impatient to enjoy his complete liberty, he bade adieu to his imbecile Mentor and his fel-low-travellers, and left Naples for Rome, from whence he intended to proceed to Venice. Elias, who had preceded his arrival at Rome, had prepared for him splendid apartments, which consoled him for the inferior accommo-dations at Naples. The most sublime objects in Rome soon lost their interest with Alfieri: his previous enthusiasm had subsided into an indifference of which he felt ashamed. While at Rome, he was presented to the Pope, Cle-ment XIII.: the dignified and venerable aspect of the Pontiff, and the splendour by which he was surrounded, reconciled the proud spirit of Alfieri to the ceremony of prostration, though his perusal of the *Ecclesiastical History* had not increased his respect for priestly supremacy.

He had applied for, and obtained leave of the
Piedmontese government to travel in France,
England, and Holland; but the joy which this
permission excited was much abated by the re-
ceipt of a letter from his guardian, refusing to
allow him more than fifteen hundred sequins a
year during his travels. This limitation of his
expenditure greatly mortified Alfieri, who had
received twelve hundred the preceding year,
and calculated on the comparative dearness of
the countries he was about to visit. He was,
however, obliged to submit, for fear his guardian
should appeal to the king, and describe him as
a spendthrift or a libertine. This sovereign
took such a lively interest in his subjects' wel-
fare, that he was perpetually meddling in their
private affairs, and Alfieri had no wish for such
a guardian. He resolved to economise his resources, that the savings of the present year's
allowance might increase his promised stipend;
and, passing from one extreme to the other, he
became on a sudden as avaricious as he had
been formerly profuse. He neglected seeing

many of the curiosities of Rome, to avoid the
trifling expense attending them, and became so
niggardly in his, allowance to his valet, that
Elias was nearly starved out of his service; but
his remonstrances, at length, produced a more
liberal supply. Setting out for Venice, in the
beginning of May, 1767, his new passion for
economy induced Alfieri to hire mules, whose
slowness he detested, in order to avoid the expense of travelling post. Unable to tolerate
the continual stumbling of these sluggish animals, he travelled the greater part of the way
on foot, calculating how much he should save
during his journey and his abode in Venice.
He had engaged the muleteer as far as Bologna,
but by the time he arrived at Loretto, he was so
overcome with ennui and disgust, that he paid
the muleteer his whole demand, and posted the
remainder of the journey. Having got the
better of this violent fit of avarice, he was
never troubled with a relapse.

Arriving at Venice, Alfieri was surprised and
delighted with the singular position of that city.

The influx of strangers, the number and gaiety of the fêtes, added to the Feast of the Ascension, detained him till the middle of June, and alleviated, for a time, the pressure of ennui. His disorder, however, soon returned, and he spent the latter part of his stay at Venice in solitude and inactivity; restless, yet incapable of exertion, and frequently bursting into tears without being able even to imagine a cause. Leaving Venice with more eagerness than he entered it, he passed through Padua, without thinking of Petrarch who lay buried so near it, and proceeded, through Vicenza, Verona, Mantua, and Milan, to Genoa, of which he had just seen enough in his former excursion to make him wish to revisit it. He had many letters of introduction, but he either neglected to deliver them, or shunned the acquaintances they procured him. Without resources in himself, which might make solitude supportable, his haughty reserve kept him aloof from society. Almost the only person with whom he was acquainted at Genoa was his banker, who, pitying

the manner in which he idled away his life, introduced him to the Chevalier Negroni, an accomplished man, and an experienced traveller.
Introduced by the latter into the first families
in Genoa, Alfieri became deeply enamoured of
an amiable female, who seemed far from averse
to his attentions; but his passion for travelling,
and his desire to escape from Italy, prevented
any permanent attachment. The description
which Negroni had given him of Paris inflamed
his desire of visiting it, and he determined to
proceed thither without farther loss of time.
He embarked in a small felucca for Antibes,
and, on landing in France, found every thing
new and delightful.

CHAPTER THE FIFTH.   1767-1768.

He visits France, England, and Holland.

FROM Antibes, he hastened to Toulon and Marseilles : he remained a month at the latter city,
attracted by the beauty of its situation, its fine
port, its straight and handsome streets, and
especially the grace and liveliness of its female
inhabitants.   He frequented a *table d'hôte* every
day, and had the satisfaction of being in society
without the labour of contributing to support a
conversation.   The company consisted chiefly
of officers and merchants, whose incessant
chattering amused him, though he never ventured to take a part in it.   The French theatre
was the principal object of interest with Alfieri,
who had fallen in with a company of French
comedians two years before, and was struck

with the superiority of their performances to
those of his own country. Their drama, however, wearied him by its cold and artificial tone,
and the interruption of the interest of the piece
by the introduction of whole scenes, and even
acts, occupied by inferior characters. He began
to feel the beauty of the Italian language, contrasted with the poverty of the French, and the
insipid uniformity of French versification. The
tragedies which pleased him most were the
Phèdre of Racine, and the *Alzire* and *Mahomet*
of Voltaire. Next to the theatre, his favourite
amusement was bathing in the sea or sitting on
the sea-shore, under a rock, from whence he
could see only sea and sky, and ruminating
with an indistinct feeling of poetical delight.
The great heats, which had detained him at
Marseilles longer than he wished, being abated,
he set off for Paris, more like a fugitive flying
for life, than a traveller in pursuit of pleasure ;
he posted day and night, without stopping, to
Lyons, where fatigue detained him for forty-
eight hours, and from thence, in less than three

days, to Paris. He entered that city in the
middle of August, on a cloudy, cold, and rainy
day, by the fauxbourg St. Marceau. Accustomed to the clear sky of Italy, the fog in
which Paris was enveloped surprised and
alarmed him. Proceeding to the fetid and miry
fauxbourg St. Germain, where he was to lodge,
his heart sunk within him, and he felt so cha-
grined at having been led into such a sink of
filth, that he would instantly have set out on his
return, had not fatigue and the fear of ridicule
opposed his retreat. The tasteless architecture
of the Parisians, their paltry houses dignified
with the titles of palaces, and, above all, the
painted faces of the women, added to his disgust, and more than counterbalanced the beauty
of their numerous gardens, the elegance of their
well-frequented promenades, their splendid
equipages, and the excellence of their theatrical
performances. The French court was passing
the autumn at Compeigne, and the Sardinian
ambassador, for whom Alfieri had letters, was
absent from the capital. Unacquainted with

any person at Paris, except a few foreigners
whom he had known in Italy, and who were as
much strangers in France as himself, Alfieri
spent his time little to his satisfaction,. at the
theatres and promenades, till the return of the
Sardinian ambassador, at the end of November,
who introduced him into Parisian society. He
began now to think of proceeding to England,
rather as a variation of wretchedness than as a
pleasurable excursion; for the disappointment
he had experienced at Paris had clouded and
saddened his anticipations. He began tardily
to appreciate his own noble country, and his
future wanderings confirmed his attachment to
it.

Before his departure for England, the Sardinian ambassador proposed to present him to the
king, and curiosity to see so celebrated a court
induced him to acquiesce. The supercilious
hauteur of the king (Louis XV.) disconcerted
and stung Alfieri, but he was consoled by seeing foreigners of much higher rank than himself
received with the same contemptuous indiffer-

ence. Alfieri set out from Paris in the middle
of January, 1768, accompanied by a young
Italian, the nephew of Prince Masserano, the
ambassador from Spain to the British court.
This gentleman was handsome, gay, and loqua-
cious : he was a great favourite with the ladies,
and delighted in recounting his love-adventures
to his taciturn companion. Alfieri was agreeably disappointed on his first arrival in England : the excellence of the roads and inns, the
beauty of the horses and the women, the neat-
ness and conveniency of the houses, the absence of mendicity, and the activity and bustle
observable in the capital and the provincial
towns, surprised and delighted him. At London,
the persuasions and example of his gay friend
drew him into the circle of fashionable dissipation. In a few months, however, he began to tire
of balls, suppers, and assemblies, and changed
his sphere of action from the drawing-room to
the coach-box. He often displayed his skill in
driving at Ranelagh and the Theatres, and prid-
ed himself on his successful dexterity in the

shock of coaches so frequent at those places.
He passed five or six hours on horseback every
morning, and two or three on the box every
evening, regardless of the weather. In the
spring, he made an excursion with his Italian
friend through the southern counties of England.
They visited Portsmouth, Salisbury, Bath, and
Bristol, and returned through Oxford to London. Pleased with the beauty of the country,
the unaffected morality of the inhabitants, the
charms and modesty of the females, and, above
all, with the freedom of thought and action
every where apparent, Alfieri was almost in-
clined to forgive the fickleness of the climate,
and the melancholy which it engendered.

Returning from this journey, which rekindled
his ardour for travelling, he left London in June
for Holland, and embarking at Harwich, with a
brisk wind, arrived in twelve hours at Helvoet-
sluys. Holland, at this time of the year, presented a pleasant and smiling aspect, and would
have pleased Alfieri had he not been previously
in England, where every thing that can be ad-

mired in this country is found in greater perfection and on a more extensive scale. During his stay at the Hague, he contrived to fall in love with a young, beautiful, and ingenuous female, who had been married nearly a year to a wealthy Hollander, the son of the Governor of Batavia. The limited society and the scantiness of amusements brought him into her company oftener than he wished, till at last he could not see her often enough. He was so fortunate as to meet with a constant and worthy friend at the Hague, Joseph D'Acunha, the Portuguese envoy, a man of a liberal and original mind, and a warm and generous heart. Happy in having some object to occupy his mind, Alfieri enjoyed for a time uninterrupted felicity in the society of his mistress and his friend. D'Acunha, perceiving the imperfect manner in which his friend's mind had been cultivated, endeavoured to turn his attention to the study of the best Italian writers in prose and verse, but without immediate success, though his labours were not ultimately fruitless. Alfieri's happiness was soon inter-

rupted: the lady's husband had purchased an
estate in Switzerland, where he was going to
pass the autumn, after making an excursion to
Spa with his wife. As the husband was not
jealous, Alfieri followed them to Spa, and accompanied them on their return as far as Maes-
tricht, where he was obliged to take his leave ;
the lady going with her mother into the country, and the husband to Switzerland. Alfieri
returned disconsolate to the Hague, where, however, he was soon agreeably surprised by the
return of the lady, who, during her absence from
her husband, had found a pretext for revisiting
that town for a few days. When the time of
departure arrived, the lady dared not trust herself to take leave of Alfieri, but set off without
his knowledge, leaving a letter for him with
D'Acunha, containing an affectionate farewell,
and explaining the necessity she was under of
immediately rejoining her husband, which could
no longer be deferred with propriety. Alfieri,
on receiving this letter, gave way to all the ex-
travagances of despair and madness, in spite of

the consolations and remonstrances of D'Acunha. Giving out that he was ill, he sent for a
surgeon, and, after being bled, dismissed his attendants, pretending to go to sleep. As soon
as the curtains were drawn he tore off the ligatures, with the intention of bleeding to death;
but his faithful Elias, suspecting some desperate resolution, suddenly withdrew the curtains,
affecting to think his master had called him.
Ashamed of his folly, Alfieri told him his ligatures had fallen off, and Elias, without showing
any disbelief, replaced them, but would not
again go out of sight. D'Acunha, informed of
this attempt, removed Alfieri to his own house,
and applied every remedy of soothing and remonstrance, but for some time without effect.
Time, however, which cures deeper wounds and
more reasonable griefs than Alfieri's, silently
and imperceptibly weaned him from his desperate resolutions. Desirous of quitting a country where every object reminded him of his mistress, he resolved to return immediately to Italy.
D'Acunha acquiesced in the propriety of his

departure, and, after taking an affectionate fare-well of this faithful friend, Alfieri set out in the middle of September to return to his native country.

Proceeding through Brussels, he traversed Lorraine, Alsace, Switzerland, and Savoy, stopping only to sleep, and perfectly indifferent to the scenes through which he passed. During the whole of this journey he scarcely opened his lips, explaining his wants by signs to Elias, who accommodated himself to all his master's humours, and answered him in the same way. After remaining six weeks with his sister at Cumiana, he accompanied her to Turin, where his acquaintances could with difficulty recognize him, so much had he increased in size and vigour during his two years' travels.

CHAPTER THE SIXTH.   1769-1770.

His short stay at Turin. His Travels in Germany, Denmark, Sweden, and Russia.   He re-visits England.

IN passing through Geneva, Alfieri had pur-chased a considerable number of publications, amongst which were the works of Rousseau, Montesquieu, and Helvetius : melancholy, and a distaste for society compelled him to have re-course to books, and he commenced his reading with the *Heloise* of Rousseau ; but after repeated attacks, he laid it down without being able to get through the first volume.   He was disgusted with the systematic affectation—the warmth of the head and the coldness of the heart—so ap-parent in every part of that celebrated work. Voltaire's prose works pleased, and his verse wearied him.   Montesquieu he read through twice with pleasure and profit. *Helvetius de l'Esprit* made a strong but disagreeable impression on his mind. But the book which charmed him beyond all others was the *Lives of Plutarch,* which he read over and over in a transport of delight, particularly the lives of Timoleon, Cæsar, Brutus, and Pelopidas. He shed tears of rage and sorrow over its pages when he recollected he was born in Piedmont, in an age which offered no scope for great deeds, and when he could only think and feel.

Alfieri's brother-in-law frequently pressed him to marry, to which he had no great aversion; but having visited England at nineteen, and read Plutarch, he disdained to settle at Turin, and beget subjects for a petty despot. He was, however, over persuaded, and suffered the Count de Cumiana to treat for a marriage betwixt him and a rich heiress of a respectable family. The lady was not averse to the match, but some of her relations objected to her union with a man of such an eccentric and ungovernable character, and his proposals, fortunately for both par-

D

ties, were rejected. The lady afterwards married a gentleman of excellent character, the favourite of the Duke of Savoy, and Alfieri was, at least, as much pleased as piqued, at the disappointment of his matrimonial arrangements.

The termination of this negociation leaving him at liberty to indulge his travelling propensities, he set out, with the king's indispensable permission, on his second journey in May, 1769, and proceeded towards Venice. He left the care of his expenditure wholly to Elias, and resolved to *think* and *observe*. *Montaigne* was his constant companion in this journey : he would frequently peruse a page or two of his *Essays*, and then meditate for hours together upon what he had read. The Latin passages, which he could not construe, frequently interrupted his reading, and even the extracts from the Italian poets were scarcely intelligible. He passed through Milan, Venice (which he had previously visited,) Trent, Inspruck, Augsburg, and Munich, almost without stopping, to Vienna. While at this city, the Sardinian Ambassador

offered to introduce him to Metastasio, but Alfieri disliked the courtly character of the poet,
and declined the honour of his acquaintance.
After making a tour in Hungary, as far as Buda,
he proceeded through Prague, to Dresden, where
he remained a month, and from thence to pass
another month at Berlin. The military despotism of Prussia was abhorrent to the fiery reader
of Plutarch, and after being presented to the
great Frederick, whom he heartily hated, he
hastened to escape from these immense barracks.
Denmark pleased him by the contrast it presented to the country he had just left, and from
the resemblance he fancied he perceived between
it and Holland. He reached Copenhagen in
December, and remained there till March, spending his time principally with some Italian noblemen, whose pure Tuscan dialect delighted him,
contrasted with the uncouth Danish. A tem-
porary illness, the result of some irregularities,
confining him to his chamber for some time,
made him renew his devotions to *Plutarch* and
Montaigne. He took great delight, when his

health permitted, in driving a sledge, the velocity
of its motion gratifying his craving for excitement.   At the end of March he set out for
Sweden, and experienced all the severity of winter as he approached Stockholm.   The novelty
and grandeur of the scenery, the savage and
majestic forests, the frozen lakes, the dreadfully
picturesque precipices—filled him with awe
and admiration.   He was not, at that time,
acquainted with *Ossian*, but some years after perusing Cesarotti's fine translation of his poems,
they recalled to his memory the scenery of Sweden in all its wild and desolate sublimity.   He
continued to amuse himself with gliding in a
sledge over the frozen lakes and plains till the
middle of April, when a sudden thaw took
place, and in four days every vestige of winter
had disappeared.

   Quitting Stockholm in the middle of May, he
visited the university of Upsal and the iron-
mines, in his way to the coast.   On his arrival
at Grisselhamn, a little port on the Gulf of Both-
nia, he found the sea partially frozen, and so

dangerous from the loose pieces of floating ice,
that no vessel could be got to carry him to
Finland. The next day, however, a fisherman
arrived from the Isle of Aland, who offered to
convey Alfieri across the Gulf, if he was willing
to encounter the hazard. Impatient of delay
he eagerly consented, and after a dangerous and
difficult voyage amidst floating masses of ice
which frequently closed upon them, and obliged
them to hew a passage with hatchets, he was
safely landed at Abo, the capital of Swedish
Finland. From thence he hastened on good
roads and with excellent horses to Petersburgh,
which he reached by the end of May, wearied,
harrassed, and bewildered by the perpetual day
of the boreal regions.

Alfieri had taken his ideas of Russia from
Voltaire's *Histoire de Pierre le Grand*, and he
was of course disappointed. Compared with
the cities he had seen, Petersburgh appeared
rather the camp of a barbarous horde, than the
capital of a powerful empire. Disgusted with
every thing belonging to these semi-barbarians,

except their beards and horses, he left Russia at
the end of June, without proceeding to Moscow
as he intended, and without being presented to
the " philosophical Clytemnestra," Catherine
the Second.

He travelled by way of Riga and Revel, over
dreary wastes, to Koningsberg and Dantzic.
Cross-examined on entering and leaving every village by a military inquisitor, respecting his name,
age, character, and pursuits, Alfieri was impatient to escape from this perpetual guard-house:
fatigue obliged him to remain three days at
Berlin: from thence he hastened through Mag-
debourg, Brunswick, Gottingen, and Frankfort,
to Mayence, where he embarked on the Rhine,
and descended that beautiful river to Cologne.
From Cologne he proceeded to Spa: this town
pleased him by its union of bustle and solitude,
affording him the pleasure of being unknown
and unnoticed amidst crowds, and fêtes, and assemblies. He spent his mornings in riding a
beautiful horse which he had purchased of an
Irishman, dined with ten or a dozen strangers,

at an ordinary, and went in the evening to see
the performances of some female dancers, He
continued at Spa from the middle of August
till the end of September, when the season being over and the place nearly deserted, he set
out for Holland, to revisit the Hague and his.
friend D'Acunha. D'Acunha received him with
open arms, and was rejoiced to find his friend a
more rational being than when he parted with
him. The lady of whom Alfieri had been enamoured, was gone with her husband to settle at
Paris. After passing two months with his friend,
he left Holland, at the end of November, for
England, which country he had an ardent desire to revisit. Arriving at London, he was wel-
comed by the friends he had acquired during
his first visit, particularly the Prince Masserano
and the Marquis Caraccioli, the Spanish and
Portuguese Ambassadors. Of the friendship
and advice of these noblemen he had the utmost need to conduct him safely through the
unfortunate events which took place during his
second residence in England.

CHAPTER THE SEVENTH.   1771.

His intrigue with Lady L ——.

ON his first visit to London, Alfieri had been
attracted by the charms of Penelope, the lady
of Viscount L——, and a lurking affection for
her had perhaps hastened his return to England.
In spite of the pangs he had suffered from his
attachment to the fair Hollander, he gave way to
this rekindled passion with all the devotedness
which might be expected from his ardent tempe-
rament. .He had frequent opportunities of seeing
Lady L—— through his intimacy with Prince
Masserano, with whose lady she shared a box
at the Opera House.   Lady L—— encouraged
his advances, and frequently admitted him to
see her at home during her Lord's absence.
In the spring Lord and Lady L— — went to re-

side for a short time at a house which his lordship had recently taken near Cobham, in Surry.
Alfieri soon after received an intimation from the
lady he might visit her on a particular day,
when her husband would be obliged to attend a
review, and to sleep in town. Alfieri set out in
the evening on horseback, unattended, and arrived in the neighbourhood of Lord L——'s residence after nightfall. He left his horse at a
small public house, between Cobham and King-
ston, proceeded on foot to his assignation, and
returned in the morning in the same manner. It
was agreed that he should visit her again in two
days' time with the same precautions. During
this interval, Alfieri's passion was wrought up to
frenzy by impatient expectation, and bewilder-
ing uncertainty, added to an irrepressible presentiment of their approaching and final separation. He spent his time in weeping and raving
in his chamber, or in galloping furiously from
place to place, and leaping over hedges and ditches at the imminent hazard of his neck. Riding
out with the Marquis Caraccioli, he observed

a very high gate, and set out at full speed to leap
over it : through the bad guidance of his bewildered and impetuous rider, the horse failed in
clearing the gate, and they both came to the
ground. Springing up immediately without feeling any hurt, Alfieri remounted his horse, who,
being again impelled to the fatal gate, cleared it
in a moment and retrieved his own and his rider's
character. But his exultation was short-lived : in
a few moments he felt an excruciating pain in his
left shoulder, and, on examination, it was found
to be broken, and his collar-bone dislocated
Surgical assistance was immediately procured,
the bones were re-set, and the patient ordered to
remain in bed. This accident occurred the day
before that he appointed for his assignation, and
his rage and anguish were boundless. He got
up at six on the appointed day, in spite of the
remonstrances of Elias, and set out alone in a
post-chaise, his ligatures, and the pain which he
suffered, rendering him unable to ride on horseback. He left the chaise at the public house he
had stopped at before, and proceeded on foot to

his rendezvous, with one arm in a sling, and
holding his sword in the other. The motion of
the chaise had deranged his bandages, and renewed the pain of his dislocation, but this did
not prevent him from thinking himself the happiest man in the world. The small gate of the
park, through which he had entered on his former
visit, he found locked, and was obliged to clam-
ber over the pales, with great pain and difficulty.
He reached the house without further interruption, and found the lady expecting him in her
apartment. He got back to London by seven in
the morning, and having had his ligatures replaced, repaired in the evening to the Opera, to
the surprise of Prince Masserano and his friends,
who little expected to see him abroad so soon
after his accident. While listening to the music with affected composure, Alfieri heard his
name pronounced in a peremptory tone at the
door of the box : rising mechanically, he opened the door and shut it after him : the first person he saw was Lord L——. The object of his
lordship's inquiry, which immediately occurred

to him, neither surprised nor grieved Alfieri.
" I am here," he exclaimed, "who asks for me?"
" It is I," said his lordship, " I wish to speak
with you,—let us walk out." "I am ready to attend you," replied Alfieri. They left the house
without further conversation, and proceeded towards the Green Park.   In walking along Pall
Mall, Lord L—— reproached Alfieri with having
entered his house clandestinely, and demanded
the reason of such conduct.   Alfieri denied the
charge, but added, that if his lordship believed it, he was perfectly ready to give him satisfaction.   Lord L—— repeated his assertion,
and detailed the particulars of the Count's last
visit with such accuracy, that the latter could no
longer doubt of his intrigue being fully discovered: his lordship added, that it was quite useless to
deny the fact, as his wife had confessed all. "If
she confesses it," replied Alfieri hastily, " why
should I deny it," and the conversation ended.
Arriving at an unfrequented part of the Green
Park, they drew their swords and prepared for
action. Lord L. observing his adversary's left

arm in a sling, offered to defer their encounter
till they could meet on more equal terms. Alfieri, thanking him for his courtesy, declared his
accident was trifling, and declined any delay.
The combat was commenced with great fury by
Alfieri, whose impetuosity and want of skill
must have rendered him a certain, if not an easy
victim, had his cooler opponent been actuated
by any very implacable revenge. After ten minutes' fighting, Alfieri received a thrust in his
right arm, between the wrist and elbow, which
he did not feel at the time. Lord L——, drop-
ping his point immediately, declared he was con-
tent with the satisfaction he had received, and,
if the Count was equally satisfied, there was an
end of the affair. The Count replying in the
affirmative, his lordship sheathed his sword,
and walked off. Alfieri on examining his
wound found it to be very slight, and, there
being no marks of blood on his clothes, he returned immediately to the company he had
quitted at the Opera. After staying there a
quarter of an hour, being unable any longer to

conceal his agitation, he left the theatre, and
hastened to the house of Lady Frances L——,
the sister-in-law of Lady L——, in hopes of
gaining some intelligence of his mistress.   To
his great surprize and joy, he there found Lady
L—— herself.   After the first transports and
inquiries of meeting were over, Lady L—— re-
counted the details of the discovery of their
connexion.   Lord L—— had learned that some
person had been clandestinely admitted into the
house during his absence, and, on his return to
town, had instructed some of his domestics to
watch for this intruder.   These servants had
seen the Count climb over the pales into the
Park, and return in the morning in the same
manner, but, seeing him armed, they did not
think fit to interrupt him.   Lord L——, in returning from town, happened to be driven by
the same postilion who had accompanied the
Count: this fellow informed him where and
what time he had waited for Alfieri, and described his person so exactly as to leave no
doubt of his identity.   Convinced of his wife's

ALFIERI.   63

dishonour, which she could scarcely persist in
denying, he declared their union at an end, and
set off immediately for London, to take vengeance on her paramour. Lady L—— immediately despatched a messenger, to inform the
Count of what had happened, who used such
expedition, that he arrived in town an hour before his lordship, but Alfieri was not to be
found. Lady L——, immediately after her husband's departure, set out for London, and proceeded to the house of her sister-in-law. In
the course of the evening, she received intelligence that Lord L—— had returned to his
house in a hackney-coach, and, in a disordered
manner, had shut himself up in his apartment.
She concluded her lover had fallen by his hand,
but, in the midst of her lamentations, Alfieri
made his appearance, as already related.

Alfieri rejoiced at this eclaircissement, as the
prelude of a divorce which would enable him to
unite himself with his mistress. Lady L——,
however, instead of sharing the joy of her lover,
appeared overwhelmed with grief. She wept

without ceasing; protesting repeatedly to Alfieri that she loved him beyond expression, and
that the dishonour and ridicule to which she
was exposed would be amply compensated by
an union with her lover—but she was sure he
would never espouse her. These exclamations,
which she continually repeated, almost distracted Alfieri; till, at length, after being repeatedly conjured to explain herself—after a
long preamble, accompanied with sighs and
tears—she confessed that she was unworthy of
his affection—that he would not, could not,
ought not to marry her—that before she had
loved him, she had loved—" Who, then ?" in-
quired Alfieri, with breathless vehemence—her
husband's groom! The agonies of a lover, and
such a lover as Alfieri, at this humiliating confession, may be more easily conceived than described. Maddening at one moment with the
wildest rage, and at the next overcome with
grief, he wept, stormed, and raved alternately.
When the first transports of his passion had
abated, he told her she had done well to con-

fess her shame : that had he married and discovered it afterwards, he would have killed her
with his own hand. Her frankness, he added, ·
had somewhat extenuated her offence, and he
would still love her—that he would accompany
her to some obscure part of Europe and America, where they might live unknown and unnoticed, but that she must never hope to be, nor
to pass for, his wife. Returning home, he threw
himself on his bed, but the tumult in his mind
prevented him from closing his eyes. Getting
up, as soon as it was light, he accidentally took
up the newspaper of the preceding day, and,
looking carelessly over it, his eye caught his
name ; reading on, he found a long and circum-
stantial account of his amour. The jealousy of
his plebeian rival, he now found, was the means
of discovering his intrigue with Lady L——,
and that this fellow was the person who revealed
it to her husband. After the discovery and duel
had taken place, the groom, in order to convince
his afflicted master how little cause he had to
regret the loss of such a wife, or actuated by an

unsatisfied spirit of revenge, informed him of
her previous infidelity. Alfieri too plainly perceived that his faithless mistress had only confessed. to him in the evening what the newspapers had published to the world in the morning.
Transported with rage, he hurried to her residence, upbraided her in the most violent manner
with her depravity and duplicity, bade her an
eternal farewell—and in less than an hour returned to console her. He continued to visit
her day after day, until Lady L——, finding
herself the talk and ridicule of the whole town,
resolved to leave London and retire to a convent
in France. Alfieri accompanied her in a tour
through England, which he suggested in order
to defer the dreaded time of separation. When
this excursion was ended, he continued to linger
with her, angry and ashamed of his weakness,
in still attaching himself to an unworthy object,
but unable to escape from her influence. At
length, in a fit of resolution, he bade her adieu
at Rochester, from whence she proceeded with
her sister-in-law to France, and the Count returned to London.

CHAPTER THE EIGHTH. 1771-1772.

He visits Spain—Returns to Italy.

LORD L—— being satisfied with obtaining a divorce from his unworthy spouse, without exacting any pecuniary compensation from her lover, there remained no obstacle to prevent Alfieri from leaving England, and he determined to quit a country where every place and every person reminded him of his folly. He embarked for Holland at the end of June, and proceeded to the Hague to join his old friend D'Acunha, with whom he remained several weeks. The necessity of volition and excitement, to dissipate the feelings which oppressed him, impelled him to re-commence his travels, and he determined to set out for Spain, the only country in Europe which he had not yet visited. Proceeding through France, he was compelled to remain a month at Paris to avoid travelling during the great heats. While at Paris, an Italian acquaintance offered to introduce him to Rousseau, whose originality and independence of character he admired, though his works fatigued and displeased him : with his usual waywardness, he declined any communication with an individual as strange and unmanageable as himself. He purchased at Paris a collection of the best Italian writers, and in the intervals of his idle fits began to study and appreciate them. Dante, Petrarch, Ariosto, Tasso, Boccaccio, and Machiavel, engrossed what little attention he bestowed on literature. Passing through France with the utmost expedition, he entered Spain by Perpignan, and made his first halt at Barcelona. He had recourse to his old favourite Montaigne for consolation on the road ; but he was much more cheered by the purchase of two beautiful Spanish horses, an acquisition he had long sighed for. Being detained some time at Barcelona by indisposition, he set about learning Spanish,

(an easy task to an Italian), and was soon able
to understand and relish Cervantes. He proceeded by the way of Saragossa to Madrid, travelling the greater part of the way on foot by
the side of his favourite Andalusian steed.
The novelty and grandeur of the scenery almost
consoled him for the badness of the inns and the
slowness of his journey. He was preceded by
Elias, on a mule, who, with his fowling-piece,
shot hares, rabbits, and birds, which he cooked
for his master's repast at their mid-day halt, or
their place of repose for the night. Alfieri remained a month at Madrid without forming
any acquaintance except with a young watchmaker, who was just returned from Holland,
where he had been to learn his trade. This
young man possessed good natural parts, and a
more liberal and cultivated mind than the generality of his countrymen.

One evening when this individual had been
supping with Alfieri, while they were yet sitting
at table, Elias began to arrange the Count's
hair, according to his custom, before going to

bed. In this operation, the valet happening to
pull one hair rather harder than the rest, his
irascible master started up, and seizing a candle-
stick, hurled it at his head : it struck him on
the right temple with such violence, that the
blood gushed out in a torrent, and covered the
watchmaker who sat on the other side of the
table. Elias rushed upon his master to take
vengeance for this outrage, but Alfieri sprang
from him, and seized his sword to defend himself. He would, however, have had little chance
of success in coping with his valet, who was of
extraordinary size and courage, but the watchmaker recovering from his surprise, threw himself between them, and the noise of the scuffle
having alarmed the house, the enraged comba-
tants were quickly parted. When the fury of
the moment had subsided, Alfieri felt deeply
ashamed and humiliated at this outrage. The
wound he had inflicted was not deep, but it bled
profusely ; had it been a little higher it would
have been fatal, and Alfieri shuddered when he
reflected that he had been so near murdering a

faithful servant for pulling a hair too hard.
Two hours after this affray, when Elias's wound
had been dressed and order restored, Alfieri
went to bed, leaving the door open as usual,
which led from his chamber to that of his valet,
in opposition to the advice of the Spaniard, who
remonstrated with him on the folly of putting
his life into the power of a justly irritated servant: to this, Alfieri replied, in a tone loud
enough for Elias to hear him, that Elias might
kill him if he pleased during the night, as he
well deserved it. The valet, however, (though
an Italian) took no other revenge than to preserve the handkerchiefs which had been bound
round his head, and sometimes to display to his
passionate master these bloody tokens of his
ungoverned temper.

Alfieri quitted Madrid in the beginning of
December, without having seen the Escurial, or
Aranjuez, or the king's palace, or the king himself. His natural indolence, and the circumstance of his being on indifferent terms with
the Sardinian envoy, whom he had known in

England, entirely repressed his curiosity. From
Madrid, he proceeded through Toledo and Ba-
dajoz to Lisbon, where he arrived on Christmas
eve.   In approaching this city from the Tagus,
he was struck by its picturesque and magnificent appearance, but the illusion was dissipated
on a nearer inspection.   Streets choked with
rubbish, tottering walls and houses in ruins,
bore witness to the ravage of the earthquake,
the traces of which the indolent Portuguese
had not suceeeded in obliterating in a lapse of
fifteen years.   During his stay of five weeks at
Lisbon, Alfieri became acquainted with the
Abbé Caluso, the younger brother of the
Count Valperga di Masino, the Sardinian ambassador.   With this accomplished and estima-
ble individual, he spent the greater part of his
time : from him, he learned to be ashamed of
the ignorance in which he had hitherto spent
his life, and which appeared more glaring and
humiliating, contrasted with the extensive eru-
dition of his companion.   The poetry which
Caluso read to him had a strong, but transient,

effect on his mind. The recitation of the Ode
to Fortune, by Guidò, (a poet, of whose existence he was till then ignorant,) excited his
enthusiasm so powerfully, that the Abbé, delighted with his ardour, felt convinced that he
was born to be a poet, and exhorted him to
turn his attention to a pursuit for which nature
had destined him. But this sudden enthusiasm
soon evaporated, and Alfieri subsided into his
accustomed listlessness. The society of the
Abbé, however, was not unproductive of improvement: he became more equable in temper
and polished in manners, and began to apply
himself, at intervals, to read, and to reflect on
what he read. Consoled, at parting, with a
promise from Caluso to meet him at Turin, he
set out at the beginning of February for Seville
and Cadiz. He was highly pleased with the
climate of Seville and the physiognomy of the
inhabitants, who have preserved more of the
original Spanish character than is seen in any
other city. After a short stay at Cadiz and at
Cordova, he traversed Valencia, delighted with

E

the pure atmosphere, the charms of the females,
and the luxuriant beauty of the country, which
seemed to realise all the fables of poetry. Arriving, for the second time, at Barcelona, he resolved to get rid of his horses, which had trotted
behind his carriage the whole of the journey,
and prevented his travelling with the rapidity he
desired. His favourite Andalusian, he presented
to a French banker at Barcelona: to this person, he afterwards applied for a letter of credit,
payable at Montpellier, in exchange for three
hundred Spanish doubloons, which the regulations of the custom-house rendered it difficult
for him to take with him. The banker took his
doubloons, and gave him a letter of credit, calculating the interest to a day; and, on his arrival at Montpellier, Alfieri found he had lost
seven per cent. by this accommodation. He
had never felt much respect for the mercantile
character, and this trait confirmed his aversion
and contempt for men of business. Posting on
without stopping to Antibes, he embarked at
that port for Genoa, from whence he proceeded

to Asti, remained a few days with his mother, and arrived at Turin on the 5th of May, 1772, after three years of absence.

CHAPTER THE NINTH. 1772-1775.

*His residence in Turin—An intrigue, and its for-
tunate termination—He commences Author.*

A DISORDER which he had contracted by
some irregularities at Cadiz, and which had
been aggravated by two months of hard travelling, obliged Alfieri to treat himself as an inva-
lid during the whole of the summer. If he
had not improved his morals or his health by
his last journey, or studied the character and
institutions of the countries through which he
had passed, yet his mind had expanded and acquired something of a more vigourous and heal-
thy tone. He was now in his twenty-third year,
rich for an inhabitant of Piedmont, vain of having seen almost every civilized country, half-
informed, overbearing, and arrogant. He had

not yet run through his long labyrinth of passion and extravagance, nor had an adequate object presented itself to his ardent and ambitious
mind. His brother-in-law vainly endeavoured
to turn his attention to diplomacy: Alfieri told
him, that he had seen enough of kings and
their deputies; that he did not care to repre-
sent the Great Mogul, much less the King of
Sardinia; and that an individual, who had the
misfortune to be born in such a country as
Piedmont, should be contented to live on his
fortune—if he had one—and to amuse himself
in a more honest manner than in soliciting a
paltry employment. This discourse visibly
lengthened the visage of the Count de Cumiana, who was a gentleman of the bed-chamber
to the king: he said no more about diplomacy,
and Alfieri enjoyed his humour unmolested.

At the end of 1773, he hired a splendid house
in Turin, and began to live in a more luxurious,
as well as a more sociable manner than hitherto,
though with a certain singularity which distinguished him from the fashionable world. He

had renewed his acquaintance with ten or a
dozen of his old companions in mirth and mis-
chief at the academy, and they established a
society, which was intended to be permanent,
with rules, oaths, and other mummeries. Their
meetings, of which the sole object was amusement, were held twice a week, and generally at
the house of Alfieri, which was more spacious
and commodious than those of his comrades.
The members were all of good families, but of
various degrees of wealth and talent. A throne
was erected in their place of meeting, through
an opening in which the members threw occasional compositions. The key of this deposi-
tory was kept by the president, who examined
the contents every week, and read them to the
society. These effusions, which were principally *jeux d'esprit*, were in the French language,
and were all anonymous. Alfieri occasionally
threw in some trifling contributions, which generally succeeded in exciting the mirth and applause of the company. Among these pieces
was a fragment descriptive of the last judge-

ment, in which the assembled souls gave an
account of their actions on earth. Several
contemporary characters were introduced which
were recognised as likenesses by the audience,
and the composition was allowed to possess
considerable truth and strength of colouring.
This essay gave Alfieri some confidence in his
powers, and inspired him with the hope of
achieving some more durable work, but a confirmed habit of indolence and self-indulgence
was not to be easily or hastily shaken off. His
horses, of whom he now possessed a dozen,
withdrew a large share of his attention from
the cultivation of those talents he had discovered in himself, and being entangled about
this time in a third intrigue, this new and violent passion absorbed, for a time, all his literary
ambition.

The object of Alfieri's attachment was a lady
of distinguished rank, but of indifferent reputation, who was nine or ten years older than himself. He had been slightly acquainted with her
during his residence at the academy, and,

though her charms were of no ordinary description, his indolence might still have baffled their influence, had not the lady herself made the first advances. The boundless affection she professed for him excited a corresponding ardour in the breast of Alfieri. His friends, his amusements, even his horses, were forgotten. From eight in the morning till midnight, he remained constantly by her side, ashamed and indignant at the servitude to which he was reduced, but without sufficient resolution to rebel against her authority. In this manner, he continued to exist for upwards of a year and half, in a state of incessant irritation, which soured his temper and undermined his health.

At the end of 1773, he was attacked by a disorder so singular, that it was said, in Turin, to have been made expressly for him. For thirty-six hours, he was afflicted with incessant vomitings, which were succeeded by convulsions so violent, that nothing could be administered to him. Though greatly reduced by illness and deprivation of food, his resistance to any attempt to hold him was greater than it could have been in perfect health. On the fifth day of his illness, his life was despaired of, and one of his friends was sent for, to advise him to be confessed and to make his will. Alfieri, divining the purport of his visit, prevented him by coolly desiring a priest and a notary might be sent for. The day after, he was placed in a warm bath of oil and water, in which he remained six hours, and was much relieved: by perseverance in this treatment, he was in a few days cured of his disorder. His long abstinence and his violent retchings had caused a hollow to form between the two bones of his breast, large enough to admit a small egg, and which continued unobliterated all his life.

This illness afforded him a pretext for resigning his commission in the regiment of Asti, to which he had now belonged eight years, and, during that time, had assisted at only four reviews. His malady had interrupted, without weakening, his devotion to his mistress, and, as soon as his health permitted, he resumed his

diurnal attendance. Ashamed of this igno-
minious subjection to the humours of a capricious woman, he shunned the society of his
most intimate friends, thinking that he read in
every countenance condemnation and contempt.
At the beginning of the ensuing year, the lady
fell dangerously ill: her disorder required uninterrupted repose and silence, and her lover,
placing himself in a chair at the foot of her
bed, remained there from morning till evening
without uttering a word for fear of disturbing
her. In one of these sittings, overcome with
weariness, he took up some sheets of paper,
which happened to lie near him, and began
writing, without any object or plan, a dialogue
in verse on the story of Cleopatra. The persons
in this shapeless sketch were Cleopatra, Photi-
nus, and a female whom he called Lachesis,
without recollecting that it was the name of one
of the Parcæ. The impulse which directed him
to this subject in preference to any other tragic
adventure, he probably owed to the impression
made on his mind by the splendid tapestry in

his mistress's anti-chamber, representing the story of Antony and Cleopatra.

The lady recovered, and Alfieri forgot his scribblings, which he had deposited under the cushion of her couch. Becoming every day more and more impatient of his bondage, he resolved to make a desperate effort to free himself, and to try if absence could not cure him of his passion. He took advantage of one of the frequent quarrels which broke out between them, and, without saying any thing of his intention, returned to his own house to make preparations for his departure from Turin. The lady heard next day of his intended flight, and returned him, according to custom, his letters and portrait. This shook his resolution, but did not overcome it. He set out manfully on the following morning, but by the time he arrived at Novara, his courage had forsaken him. He sent on his equipage and a French Abbé, whom he had hired to attend him on this journey, to Milan, with directions to wait there for his arrival. Mounting his horse, he travelled all night on his way back, and, by day-break, found himself within sight of Turin. Ashamed to enter the city in the day-time, he stopped at a paltry inn in the suburbs, and despatched a penitent epistle to his mistress, entreating her forgiveness and an immediate audience. A favourable answer was brought him by Elias, who was left at Turin to superintend the Count's affairs in his absence, and who was always indefatigable in endeavouring to conceal his master's follies from the world. After night-fall, Alfieri stole into the city to his assignation, and received a free pardon on his unconditional submission. It was agreed, that he should resume his travels for four or five weeks, and then return under pretence of ill health. Peace being thus settled, Alfieri again sallied forth for Milan, bitterly regretting his vacillation, and cursing the fatal influence to which he had so weakly submitted. At one moment, he revolved every means to prolong his absence, without violating his promise, and the next how to shorten it, without rendering himself publicly ridiculous.

Seeking refuge from reflection in velocity of
motion, he staid only two days at Milan, and
from thence hurried to Modena, Bologna, Florence, Pisa, and Leghorn. At the latter place,
he received letters from his mistress, and, unable to endure any longer the torments of absence, he turned his course homewards. Leaving at Genoa his carriage and his French Abbé,
he took horse, and arrived at Turin, eighteen
days after having quitted it for a journey of
twelve months. He entered the city, as before,
at night, to avoid the observations and jests of
the fashionable world, and, by his austere and
sombre demeanour, endeavoured to baffle the
ironical congratulations of his ill-natured
friends. Several months had elapsed in this
state of irksome restraint, when, returning one
evening from the Opera, where he had passed
some hours in the company of his adored and
hated mistress, he determined to make another
and more desperate effort to recover his freedom. He had experienced the inutility of
flight, and now deemed it best to meet and

brave the danger. The lady's house faced his
own, and he resolved to see her go in and out,
and to hear her voice, and yet remain unmoved,
either by messages, direct or indirect, intreaty
or threat, or even by indifference. To cut off
all means of retreat, he wrote to one of his
most esteemed friends, informing him of the
step he had taken, and inclosing a lock of his
long red hair, which he had cropped to preclude
his appearing abroad, as none but peasants and
sailors wore their hair short. He passed the
first five days of his seclusion in giving vent to
tears and groans. Distrusting the obduracy of
his resolution, he caused himself to be tied
down in his chair, leaving one hand at liberty
to read or write, and concealing the cords by a
large cloak in which he was wrapped. No one
was aware of this restraint except Elias, who
officiated as his goaler, and untied him when he
appeared tolerably rational and temperate. He
endeavoured to study, but he could not command attention sufficient to comprehend what
he perused, and read over page after page aloud,

without recollecting a word. Sometimes he
ventured out on horseback, chusing the most
unfrequented places for his excursions. Two
months passed away in this manner, leaving
him in a state bordering on frenzy, when one
day it occurred to him that the composition of
poetry might divert the current of his thoughts;
and, sitting to work, he strung together, with
great labour and difficulty, fourteen lines, which
he called a sonnet. This effusion he shewed to
one of his friends, the learned Father Paciaudi,
who compassionately visited him from time to
time, in the hope of interrupting his melancholy
reveries. Paciaudi bestowed on this jejune
composition praises which he knew it did not
deserve; but which had the desired effect of
turning Alfieri's serious attention to composition. Some days before his rupture with his
mistress, he happened to recollect the *Cleopatra*
which he had left under the cushion of her
couch a year before, and rescued it from its
long immurement. In one of his solitary pa-
roxysms, he chanced to cast his eye on it; and,

struck with the resemblance between his own
feelings and those of Antony, he resolved to
finish it and to develope the passions which
tortured him. He set to work immediately (already half cured of his malady) scribbling,
blotting, altering, adding, and subtracting, with
infinite assiduity. So anxious was he for the
success of his new enterprise, that even his
pride gave way, and he submitted to consult
such of his friends as had not, like himself,
neglected the study of the Italian language and
poetry, and teased them incessantly for their
advice and opinions. His house appeared like
an academy, and, from the most unmanageable,
he became, all at once, the most docile of mor-
tals. The ambition of learning overcame every
obstacle of arrogance and indolence, and his
love was absorbed by this new and master passion. He had no longer any occasion to be tied
down in his chair. One of his latest freaks was
to appear in the character of Apollo at a public
ball in the Theatre, with a lyre, on which he
played as well as he could, which was very in-

differently, and sung some sorry verses of his own composing. This exhibition was quite at variance with his character and habits, and seemed adopted to give some public display of his emancipation, and to render the breach between himself and his mistress irreparable. The passion for literary distinction continued to excite him to such exertions, that, after many poetical consultations, ransacking grammars and dictionaries, and scribbling and erasing abundance of nonsense, he managed to produce a tragedy in five acts. As soon as one act was finished, it was despatched to the polite Father Paciaudi, for his critical examination. Some of his marginal remarks made Alfieri laugh, though at his own expense. *" The barking of the heart"*—" This metaphor," observed the Abbé, " smacks of the dog :—pray, take it away." The Count Augustin Tana, one of the academical friends of Alfieri, and of his own age, assisted him greatly by his ingenious and just observations on this shapeless production. The advice of his two friends induced the young

bard to re-write the whole of his work, which
he set about with great patience and industry.
This laborious task was at last completed, and
Cleopatra was produced at the theatre of Turin,
June 16, 1775. After the tragedy, was performed a short piece in prose, which Alfieri had
written for the occasion, entitled *The Poets.* In
this, he introduced himself under the name of
Zeuzippe, and ridiculed the defects of his *Cleopatra.* These dramas, though indifferent in the
conception, and worse in the execution, were
evidently the productions of a powerful mind,
which only wanted judicious cultivation to
bring forth nobler fruits. They were received
with great indulgence, but their author, now
more sensible of their defects, and repenting
his temerity, caused them to be withdrawn after
the second representation.

CHAPTER THE TENTH. 1775-1777.

His literary labours, and the difficulties he had to encounter.

ALFIERI was twenty-seven when he commenced author. His only guide in this undertaking was a vague recollection of the French tragedies he had seen some years before, but which he had neither read nor studied—and his principal support, a resolute, confident, and inflexible character, animated by a boundless feeling of love, and a more boundless hatred of tyranny. Ignorant of the rules of dramatic composition, and of the method of writing his own language with clearness and precision, he had almost every thing to learn, and, with a temper which could ill brook the laborious detail of study, he found that he must retrace his steps, return to his grammar, and resume the docility and drudgery of the school-boy. This was a bitter and humiliating necessity, but his new-born enthusiasm was too powerful to allow him to shrink from the task. The Italian—the most musical, flexible, and poetical of modern dialects, equally susceptible of the impression of softness or of strength, of languid diffuseness or of vigourous compression—is rather a written than an oral language. It is commonly distinguished as the *Florentine* or the *Tuscan* dialect; but as the most rigourous verbal critics admit many words to be correct and classical, which are current neither in the capital nor the territory of Tuscany, this designation is incorrect, or at least not sufficiently comprehensive. The Italian is an ideal language, which has the Tuscan for its base, but which receives and naturalizes recruits from all the provinces of Italy, and (as it has been observed by one of their eminent writers*) is to be found every where in parts, but no where as a

* Monti.

whole. · This ideal character, while it renders it
a more delightful vehicle for the poetry of imagination, necessarily circumscribes the resources
of the dramatist, and the want of a precise
standard of idiomatic phraseology precludes the
attainment of excellence in familiar humour and
comic dialogue. Goldoni, by birth a Venetian,
and instructed betimes in the written language
of the Peninsula, who had passed six years of
his life in Tuscany, and had written thirty-one
octavo volumes in Italian, never attained the
art of composing in it with purity, force, and
precision. He went to France at an advanced
period of life, and, after a few years' residence
there, wrote a comedy in French, which was
well received, and of which the language was
sufficiently correct to escape criticism. The
Galateo of Casa, the most perfect model of Italian elegance and purity, is said to have occupied its author thirty or forty years in its composition, yet the matter could hardly have cost
him the labour of as many hours.

Alfieri entered upon his dramatic career with-

out being aware of half the difficulties he had
to encounter, and to this ignorance may be
traced his temerity, his perseverance, and his
ultimate success. A more refined taste and a
greater intimacy with the best models might
have repressed emulation by despair, or re-
strained his genius within the limits of correct
mediocrity. In the unreflecting enthusiasm of
the moment, he had struck out a piece, which,
crude and imperfect as it was, was crowned
with a success which promised an ample meed
of applause for his more mature and perfect
productions.

Three months before *Cleopatra* was produced
at the theatre, Alfieri had written two tragedies
in French prose, *Philip* and *Polinices*. He read
them to several friends, who not only praised
them, but appeared interested and affected by
their recital; but when he rendered a scene or
an act into Italian, it appeared enervated and
spiritless, and the same audience which had applauded it in French could scarcely believe it
to belong to the same work in Italian. A habit

of speaking and thinking in French during five
years of travelling, had given him a facility and
power of expression in that language which he
could not command in his own. He resolved
to unlearn his French as fast as possible, and to
clothe all his thoughts in Italian. He began to
exercise himself in every species of poetical
composition, and in every variety of metre.
Among other attempts, he composed some
couplets which he sung at a meeting of free-
masons, who, understanding as little of the
structure of verse as of buildings, applauded
this effusion, though very poor in sense and
lame in metre. Finding that the dissipation of
the city prevented his bestowing undivided attention to his studies, he retired, in August, to
Cezannes, a little village among the mountains
which separate Piedmont from Dauphiné. It
did not occur to him that he should there encounter the hated French language, and he even
engaged as his companion the French Abbé,
who had attended him on his last inglorious
expedition. This Abbé, who was a native of

Cezannes, was a philosopher and a man of taste, and perfectly conversant with French and Latin literature. Besides his literary Abbé, Alfieri took with him to this retreat a musical Abbé, who taught him to play on the guitar; but though passionately alive to the influence of sweet sounds, he continued a very indifferent musician. He began to naturalize his two tragedies in Italian prose, but, in spite of his pains, they retained something of their mongrel origin. He re-wrote his *Cleopatra* for the third time: he had read some scenes of this play to Count Tana, who pronounced them fine and forcible, particularly that between Antony and Augustus; but when transformed into dry and nerveless Italian verse, he condemned them as below mediocrity. After having translated his tragedies into bad prose, he began to read and study, verse by verse, the most eminent Italian poets, marking such passages as appeared to him superior to the rest in the thought, expression, or cadence. He found Dante too difficult, and quitted him for Tasso: he afterwards read the *Orlando,* then returned to Dante, and lastly studied Petrarch. But, as his object was to excel in blank verse, he began to look for models in that style of composition. He was advised to study Bentivoglio's translation of Statius, and perused it with great avidity ; but the structure of the verse appeared to him too feeble for dramatic dialogue. Cesarotti's translation of Ossian he thought a much better model, and that, with some alterations, it would answer his purpose. The *Merope* of Maffei pleased him in parts, but its style fell far short of his ideas of dramatic excellence. Determined to avoid the diffuseness and languor which characterised the poets of the preceding generation, he went at once to the opposite extreme, and became systematically harsh in his style and versification. After spending six months in the study of Italian, Alfieri was seized with shame at being ignorant of Latin. He had seen some fragments of Seneca's tragedies, and was anxious to become acquainted with the whole of them, as well as the Latin translations of the

F

Greek tragedians, which were considered more
faithful than the Italian. Having provided himself with an excellent master, he applied patiently to re-learn his Latin, and, after three
months of hard labour, became a tolerable pro-
ficient in that language. He had versified his
Philip, but, though superior to the *Cleopatra*, it
was still languid and prolix. This play con-
tained upwards of two thousand lines, though
he afterwards reduced it to fourteen hundred.
Finding the odious French language still cling
to his tongue and his imagination, he determined to remove into Tuscany, and to accustom
himself to speak and think only in Tuscan. He
set out from Turin in April, 1776, with a small
retinue and very little luggage, on this literary
expedition. He was introduced by Father Paciaudi to most of the literary men of the cities
he visited, and he now courted their acquaintance as assiduously as he had formerly shunned
it. For some months, he kept a regular journal
of all he did and learned, of his follies, and
even of his thoughts. During a stay of six or

seven weeks at Pisa, he formed the plan of his *Antigone*, which he wrote in Italian prose. He versified *Polinices*, and afterwards read it to some of the principal professors of the university, who bestowed more praise upon it than its author could believe it deserved. He also translated Horace's *Art of Poetry*, in order to familiarize himself with its precepts, and began to study the tragedies of Seneca, which pleased him much, in spite of their transgressions against the rules of Horace, and translated portions of them into blank verse. The perusal of Seneca suggested the subjects of the tragedies of *Agamemnon* and *Orestes*, which he commenced soon after, but his manner of handling the story was original. He had hitherto taken the first idea of his tragedies from other plays, but he now determined to rely on his own resources, and, in adherence to this resolution, gave up reading the plays of Shakspeare, which he had just commenced in a French version. In proportion as he was pleased with this author, he thought it the more necessary to abandon him.

At the end of June, he left Pisa for Florence, where he remained two months, using every means of perfecting himself in the beautiful dialect of that capital, and employing himself in versifying his *Philip* for the second time. Hearing in a company of literary men some mention of the tragical death of Don Garcia, by the hand of his father, Cosmo I. he was struck with the account, and conceived the plot of his tragedy on that subject.   He returned to Turin in October, not because he thought himself sufficiently *Tuscanized*, but from his not having made arrangements for a longer absence. His horses too were a powerful attraction to draw him home : indeed, his horsemanship had frequently struggled hard for mastery with his devotion to the Muses.   In spite of the temptations of pleasure and friends which surrounded him at home, he continued to pursue his studies with increasing activity.   Charmed with the precision and elegance of Sallust, he set about translating his history, and accomplished his task during the winter. This translation, he several times subsequently corrected and polished.

While Alfieri was thus engaged, his friend Caluso, returning from Portugal, was agreeably surprised to find him immersed in literature, and encouraged him with his advice and assistance to persevere. About this time, he received the first and most gratifying reward of his exertions. Repairing one morning to Count Tana (to whom he always took his compositions as soon as written) with a sonnet, the Count on reading it, exclaimed—" These are the first of your verses which are worthy of you." This spontaneous tribute of sincere praise filled Alfieri with transport, and amply compensated him for the labour and humiliating tasks he had submitted to. This sonnet was a description of the carrying off of Ganimede, in imitation of Cassiani's fine sonnet on the rape of Proserpine. Encouraged by the success of this effusion, Alfieri wrote

many other sonnets, principally amatory, which
were, however, but exercises of the imagination,
and not dictated by love. In the spring, he
versified his *Antigone*, completing this task in
three weeks, with increasing facility : but, after
reading it to some friends, he was convinced
that his improvement was not so apparent as he
had expected. He discovered in this piece
abundance of false and feeble thoughts, and expressions deficient in force, conciseness, and
elegance. He resolved immediately to leave
Turin, convinced that the Piedmontese jargon
which was spoken there, was as hostile to the
Italian as the French itself. On applying for
the King's gracious leave of absence, the Minister to whom he applied himself observed,
that he had been in Tuscany the preceding
year. Alfieri replied, that that was the exact
reason why he wished to return thither. The
desired permission was granted, but the accompanying demur was highly offensive to the ungovernable spirit of Alfieri; and this interview
suggested to him a scheme of emancipation,

which a few months after he carried into execution. He intended to remain some time in Tuscany; and, mingling a little vanity with his passion for literature, he resolved to take with him a numerous train of horses and servants. He wished to act the parts, rarely united, of a poet and a great man. With eight horses and a proportionate suite, he set out in May for Genoa. Embarking there, with his carriage and luggage, he sent on his horses by land to Lerici and Sarzana. When within sight of Lerici, a contrary wind rose and drove him back to Rapolo, which is within two stages of Genoa. Disembarking at Rapolo, and being soon weary of waiting for a favourable wind, he left his luggage on board the felucca, and taking his portfolio (from which he never parted) he set out, accompanied by a single domestic; traversed the precipices of the Apennines, and arrived at Sarzana eight days before the felucca. Having only a Horace and a Petrarch in his pocket, the time passed away heavily, even with the company of his stud of horses, which he found at Sarzana. He borrowed from a priest a copy of Livy, an author whom he had not met with since he left the Academy. Though a passionate admirer of the brevity of Sallust, he was struck with the majesty and sublimity of Livy. The story of Virginius and the glowing speeches of Icilius delighted him, and he immediately conceived the plot of a tragedy on this subject, but the arrival of the felucca interrupted its immediate completion.

The tragedies of Alfieri went through three distinct processes, which he entitled, *conception, developement,* and *versification.* To *conceive* was to arrange the subject in acts and scenes, fix the number of characters, and write a summary of what they were to do and say: to *develope, to* write the dialogue in prose, without rejecting any thought that occurred, and delivering himself up to the inspiration of the moment, without any regard to correctness. The third process consisted not only in putting the dialogue into verse, but in selecting, lopping, adding, and condensing, and giving to the whole a

more poetical form. After these three operations were completed, he revised and polished
the work at his leisure. If on returning to his
subject, after having *conceived* and *developed* it,
he did not find himself actuated by the same
enthusiasm, he abandoned it altogether: a tragedy of *Charles I.* and another of *Romeo and
Juliet,* were thrown aside for this reason, after
having gone through the first and second process. It was Alfieri's favourite object, and one
which he never lost sight of, to preserve an
uniformity and consistency from the beginning
to the end of each play: to dove-tail the scenes
into each other, so that their juxta-position
could not be altered without ruining the plot;
and to preserve a continuity in the style and
sentiments, and imagery, as well as in the action.

From Lerici, he proceeded to Pisa, where he
remained but two days, and hastened on to
Sienna, partly because the Tuscan was spoken
more correctly at the latter place, but chiefly
to avoid a lady whom he had seen at Pisa the

year before, and whom he was afraid of falling
in love with. Her person, character, and family, were unexceptionable, but his passion for
study, and a conviction that he could not write
or speak with the freedom essential to his literary independence, if encumbered with a wife
and children, determined him to resist her at-
tractions. At Sienna, he was introduced into
a circle of five or six individuals of taste and
judgment. Among these was Francis Gori Gandellini, with whom he contracted a friendship,
which ended only with the life of the latter.
Alfieri fancied he saw in Gandellini a strong
resemblance to his own character and manner
of thinking, united with more amenity, extensive learning, and an enlarged mind. This
friend suggested to him the conspiracy of the
Pazzi as a fit subject for a tragedy, and advised
him to consult Machiavel for the details. Alfieri
was so much delighted with this nervous and
original writer, that after arranging the plot of
his tragedy, he laid it aside to read and imitate
Machiavel. This course of study produced his

two books, *Della Tirannide*, a series of close arguments and severe remarks on monarchy. Laying aside this diatribe, after reading it to a few of his friends, he resumed the cothurnus, and developed with rapidity, *Agamemnon*, *Virginia*, and *Orestes*. After passing five months at Sienna to his great satisfaction and improvement, he removed to Florence, intending to make a short stay there, but circumstances subsequently occurred which induced him to make that city his place of residence for many years.

CHAPTER THE ELEVENTH.   1777-1778.

*His acquaintance with the Countess of Albany—
Sacrifice of his property—Continuation of his
literary labours.*

DURING his visit to Florence, the preceding
year, he had frequently seen the Countess of
Albany, a Princess of the House of Stolberg, the
wife of Charles Edward Stuart, better known
as the young Pretender. Though charmed with
her person and manner, Alfieri shunned being
introduced to her, as most strangers were; and
contented himself with seeing her at the pro-
menade and public diversions. The Countess
was in her twenty-fifth year, handsome, amiable,
and accomplished, and rendered more interesting
by her domestic unhappiness. The early history
of the unfortunate prince, her husband, is too

well known. On the death of his father, the
Court of France reduced the pension it allowed
the royal exile, from twenty-four thousand
crowns, to eighteen thousand. Charles Edward
would not accept less than had been paid to his
father, and consequently received nothing. Spain
had promised him as large a revenue as France,
and therefore gave nothing. A pensioner on
the bounty of Churchmen, his character seemed
to fall with his fortune. He gave way to ebriety
in the company of his drunken followers; became gross and brutal in his manners, and harsh
and insolent to his immediate dependants. Illiterate and ill-informed, he retired, on every new
vexation, to consult Nostradamus, and continued, from the interpretation of his prophecies,
to flatter himself with the hope of ascending the
throne of his ancestors. Previous to his marriage, he kept a Mrs. Walkenshaw, a woman of
vulgar manners, and, like himself, habitually
drunken; they often quarrelled, and sometimes
fought, and exposed themselves, not only to
their own family, but to their neighbours. Ra-

ther than part with this woman, who was suspected to be in the pay of the British Government, and for whom he did not entertain the
slightest affection, he offended, and lost the
services of his most faithful and able adherents.

. Alfieri was first introduced to the Countess in
the great gallery of Florence, and this circumstance afforded him an opportunity of giving a
whimsical proof of his gallantry. The Countess,
in looking at a picture of Charles XII. happened
to observe that she thought that the singular
uniform, in which he was represented, extremely
becoming. Two days after, Alfieri appeared in
the streets, in the exact costume of the Swedish
hero, to the surprise and consternation of the
sober inhabitants. After struggling unsuccess-
fully for a time with this new passion, he gave
himself up to its influence, and applied himself
assiduously to cultivate the friendship of the
Countess and her superannuated husband. This
last attachment, however, was less violent, though
more intense than the preceding ones. Instead
of interrupting his studies, it added a new and

delightful incentive: her taste was a guide to his labours, and her approbation their most valued reward. He resolved not to leave Florence while the object of his affection remained there, and in consequence determined on carrying into execution a scheme, which he had for some time meditated.

He had long considered the ties which attached him to Piedmont, as an insupportable restraint, particularly the custom which obliged the possessors of fiefs to obtain leave of absence from the king, on going abroad; this permission, which was only for a limited time, was seldom obtained without difficulty, and was always granted with a bad grace. This circumstance, and the conviction that he could never print his works with safety, while subject to the laws of Sardinia, combined with his new attachment, determined him to expatriate. He might have got his permission renewed from year to year, but this state of uncertainty and dependence he could not submit to, and such an arrangement would have kept him under the control

of the Sardinian censorship. There was no way
of transferring his fortune to another country,
except in an illegal and clandestine manner, and
to such a proceeding Alfieri could not stoop:
he decided on sacrificing his property, rather
than compromise his principles or independence,
and, this resolution once taken, he lost no time
in carrying it into effect. He made over his
possessions to his sister, the Countess of Cumiana, in the most solemn and irrevocable manner,
reserving a yearly allowance of fourteen thousand
livres, which was about half his previous income.
The King's consent was indispensable to this
transfer; but his brother-in-law was too much
interested, not to exert himself, and he obtained
leave to accept the donation, as well as to pay
Alfieri his annuity, in any country he might
choose for his residence. The political sentiments of Alfieri were well known at Turin, and
it was obvious that he had some other reason
for this sacrifice, than mere change of place; but
the king, or his advisers, probably thought it
best to get rid of such a restless subject.

Though he had taken such a desperate step to free himself from the controul of his Sardinian Majesty, he continued, with a whimsical inconsistency, to wear his uniform for four years after he had quitted the army, because he fancied it became him. The necessary arrangements, and the legal formalities and procrastinations, protracted the discussion of his affairs from January till November, 1778, and harrassed and irritated him beyond measure. The settlement was still farther delayed by Alfieri's wishing to receive the sum of one hundred thousand livres, in lieu of a yearly annuity of five thousand livres. The consent of the king to this second arrangement was at length obtained, and Alfieri placed this, with other sums, in the French funds. He said nothing to the Countess of the sacrifice he was making to enjoy her society, till it was carried into effect, that her disinterested friendship might not oppose his romantic design. She blamed his precipitancy, as he expected; but finding it was too late to prevent his imprudent project, she did not trouble him with remon-

strances, and was probably not displeased at an
extravagance, of which she could not but guess
the motive. While Alfieri was writing letter
after letter to Turin, to remove the obstacles
which the king, the law, and his relations, threw
in the way of the adjustment of his affairs, he
had given orders to Elias, who remained at
Turin, to dispose of his plate and other movea-
bles, being resolved to adhere to his scheme of
enfranchisement, let what would happen. Elias
set to work diligently, and in two months time
realized six thousand sequins, by the sale of his
property, which his master directed him to remit
to him at Leghorn. By some accident, the re-
mittance was delayed three weeks, during which
time, Alfieri received no letter from Elias, or any
other person in Piedmont: though not of a sus-
picious nature, he began to apprehend that his
valet had disappeared with his sequins; this
conjecture was the more alarming, as his arrangements with his sister were not concluded, owing
to the chicanery of her husband, and he had
written to the latter a peremptory and defying

letter, insisting on the negociation being concluded, and expressing his determination to expatriate, though it were as a beggar. In the anxious interval which ensued, with the prospect of
approaching poverty, Alfieri revolved the means
of earning an independent livelihood, and the
most feasible appeared to be the profession of a
horse-breaker, for which he thought himself extremely well qualified. These chimerical dis-
tresses were however soon put an end to by the
arrival of the bills of exchange from Elias.

As soon as the act of donation was passed,
Alfieri dismissed all his domestics, except one.
He accustomed himself to the strictest tempe-
rance and sobriety, abstaining entirely from wine,
coffee, and similar luxuries, and confining himself to the most simple food. For several years
he subsisted entirely on baked or boiled rice.
He sold or gave away his fine stud of horses, bestowed his rich dresses on his valet de chambre,
and resigned his cherished uniform. He chose
a dark blue dress for the morning, which he exchanged for black in the evening, and adhered

to these colours for the remainder of his life. After giving away half his property, he felt so anxious to improve the remainder, that he became parsimonious in his manner of living, and was continually inventing new methods of economy and privation. The acquisition of books was the only expensive pursuit in which he indulged; he collected all the standard Italian works, and many of the Latin classics, of the best and finest editions. The society of the Countess presented an obstacle to the favourite object of Alfieri's ambition, the mastery of the Italian, since from her ignorance of that language he was obliged to converse with her in French. His repeated persuasions induced her to learn Italian, and she soon acquired the language so completely, that her pronunciation was as correct as that of any Italian lady, who was not a native of Tuscany.

In 1778, after having versified *Virginia*, and nearly the whole of *Agamemnon*, he was attacked by a severe illness, the result of the agitation he had experienced from his domestic embarrass-

ments, his study, and his love. As soon as he
was sufficiently recovered, he renewed his literary labours with unabated zeal. He wrote a
poem on the death of Duke Alexander, killed by
Lorenzino de Medici, as well as several amatory
pieces, in which he delineated the passion he
felt, and his grief for the unhappy situation in
which its object was placed. In the course of
the year, he sketched the plots of his tragedies
of the *Pazzi* and *Don Garcia*, versified his
Orestes, and commenced a tragedy on the subject of *Mary Stuart*, at the suggestion of the
Countess. He also conceived, and divided into
chapters, his three books of *Il Principe e le Lettere*, a work written to prove that poets, histori-
ans, and orators, can flourish only in a free state.

CHAPTER THE TWELFTH.   1779-1782.

*Separation of the Countess from her husband.—
Alfieri completes twelve of his tragedies.*

ALFIERI, at this part of his life, spent almost
the whole of the day in his study, going out for
a short ride, in the morning, for his health, and
in the evening he visited the Countess and her
disagreeable husband. In this manner his days
passed, in an almost uninterrupted calm, enlivened by the society of the Countess, and the
letters from his friends, among whom Caluso and
Gandellini held the highest rank.   His second
fit of avarice had insensibly worn off: he had
resumed a liberal, but still a moderate expenditure, and had purchased four horses, which however he regarded as too many for a poet.   His
principal in the French funds amounted to one

hundred and sixty thousand livres, and he con-
gratulated himself on having secured a compe-
tent maintenance, independent of his Piedmontese annuity. The only interruption to his
tranquillity resulted from the domestic unhappiness of the Countess, whose husband became
every day more drunken and peevish. His ill
humour was probably little alleviated by the attentions of Alfieri to his wife, though their intimacy was confined within the limits of the
strictest decorum. Indeed, Alfieri was unable
to see the Countess, except at dinner, or in the
evening, when the husband was always present,
or in an adjoining room, not so much from any
jealousy the latter entertained of him, as from its
being his custom. During the nine years the
Countess had been married to him, he had never
been out without her, or she without him.

In the course of 1779, he conceived the tragedies of *Timoleon* and *Octavia*, the subject of
the one taken from *Plutarch*, and the other inspired by *Tacitus*. He developed *Mary Stuart*,
conceived and developed *Rosmunda*, versified.

Don Garcia, and the *Conspiracy of the Pazzi;*
finished the first book of his poem of *Etruria
Vindicata,* and made some progress in the second.
In the following year he developed *Timoleon* and
Octavia, and versified *Philip* for the third time,
abridging it considerably. He also versified
Mary Stuart, Rosmunda, and a great part of
Octavia.

The ill treatment which the Countess experienced from the brutality of her husband becoming more intolerable every day, and her health
being visibly on the decline, it became necessary
to find means of rescuing her from his tyranny.
Alfieri was thus impelled to adopt a course
which he detested, and to engage in intrigues
with those who had interest with the government, to effect the separation of the Countess
from her husband. The ill-usage and restraint
to which she had long been subjected, and which
was gradually ruining her health, were sufficiently notorious, and Alfieri was ultimately successful in his application. The Countess, on
receiving this welcome intelligence, went, as

was arranged, to visit one of the Convents of
Florence : her husband, as usual, accompanied
her, but was greatly astonished when informed
that she was to remain there, by order of Government. This abrupt desertion deeply affected
the unhappy prince, and he endeavoured by
every concession to win her back. Finding his
efforts ineffectual, he was persuaded to recall his
daughter, by Mrs. Walkenshaw, to whom his
previous conduct had been cruel and unnatural.
He had revenged on this unfortunate girl the
desertion of her mother, and now his returning
fondness was as extravagant as his former aversion. The Countess did not remain long in the
retreat she had chosen ; she was sent for, to
Rome, by her brother-in-law, Cardinal York, to
be placed in a Convent, in that city.

Alfieri remained behind, disconsolate and
helpless : he felt himself incapable of any occupation, his studies were abandoned, and even
his love of fame forgotten. Propriety forbade
him to follow the Countess to Rome, and he
believed it impossible for him to exist in Flo-

G

rence. To add to his distress, his friend Caluso,
who had resided, during the preceding twelve
months, at Florence, and passed the greater part
of his time in his company, was under the necessity of returning to Turin. After lingering
at Florence for a month after the departure of
the Countess, he determined to visit Naples, an
excursion which would oblige him to pass
through Rome. He set out on this journey the
beginning of February, 1781, and visited Sienna
in his way, to embrace his friend Gandellini.
On his arrival at Rome he hastened to visit the
Countess, and was allowed to see her through
the grate of the convent. He found her com-
paratively well and tranquil: she was no longer
persecuted by the presence of a drunken husband, who followed her like her shadow, and
this reflection alone made their separation supportable to Alfieri. During his short residence
at Rome, love made him submit to artifices,
which his proud spirit would have spurned on
any other consideration. He visited and paid
his court to the Cardinal York, on whom the

restoration of his mistress's liberty depended, and who continued to flatter him with hopes. The Cardinal was a warm-hearted, hospitable, but testy man, peremptory in his manners, and of a slender capacity. Alfieri recommenced his journey in a few days, according to his original plan, which neither prudence nor delicacy would allow him to swerve from. The sight of Naples and its beautiful environs did not divert his grief, as he anticipated. His books wearied him—his verses and his plays were neglected; his existence seemed to depend on the punctual arrival of letters from his fair friend, and to read these over a hundred times, and to write voluminous answers, formed his only amusement and consolation. At the end of March the Countess obtained, from the Pope, permission to leave the convent, and to live separate from her husband in an apartment assigned her in the house of Cardinal York. Alfieri felt impatient to rejoin her, though convinced that he ought not, and after debating between love and prudence for a month, he set out on his return to Rome.

After so many sacrifices and struggles to free
himself from the trammels of authority, love
obliged him, against his nature, to play the
courtier, visiting, caressing, and flattering the
priests and priestlings, who intermeddled with
the affairs of the Countess. Happily, she was
not dependent on her brother-in-law for support,
being possessed of an ample fortune, which was at
her own disposal. When the necessity of his
exertions was in some measure removed, and he
was at liberty to pass his evenings in the society of the Countess, he applied himself with
re-kindled ardour to his literary pursuits. He
fixed his residence at the Villa Strozzi, a delightful retreat, near the Baths of Dioclesian. He
devoted his mornings to unremitting study,
except an hour or two passed in riding in the
poetical solitudes of the environs, where every
spot was hallowed with some recollection, to
move the mind to meditation, or to kindle it to
enthusiasm. In the evening he repaired into
the city, to enjoy the conversation of the
Countess, and returned punctually at eleven

o'clock, to his solitude. It was impossible to find, within the bounds of a large city, a spot more retired, yet more cheerful, than the one he had chosen, uniting the convenience of the town with the seclusion of the country. After having finished versifying *Polinices*, he exerted himself without interruption to complete his *Antigone*, *Virginia, Agamemnon, Orestes, the Pazzi, Garcia*, and *Timoleon*, and revised, for the fourth time, his early tragedy of *Philip*. As a relaxation from his dramatic studies, he proceeded with the third canto of his *Etruria Vindicata*, and in a fit of political enthusiasm he struck out the four first odes on the independence of America. At the commencement of 1782, he found his tragedies in such a state of forwardness, that, he hoped to finish them during the year. He had conceived, developed, and versified twelve plays, and it was his intention not to exceed that number. He continued assiduously to revise, abridge, and polish them. While thus employed, the *Merope* of Maffei happened to fall in his way, for the second time; and on re-perusing it,

he felt indignant at the blindness of his countrymen, in considering this play as a model of tragic excellence. It struck him forcibly that the
subject afforded materials for a much nobler
drama, more simple in its construction, and
more impassioned in its execution. This impulse produced his tragedy of *Merope,* which he
completed with a rapidity which surprised him.
He had usually allowed a considerable interval
of time to elapse between the different processes
to which he subjected his pieces, but in this in-
stance, he never laid aside his work till it was
completed. His *Saul* was produced in the
same manner. About this time he began to
study the Sacred Writings, but without any
method or regularity. He felt irresistibly impelled by their perusal to attempt a tragedy on a
sacred subject, and conceived, developed. and
versified *Saul,* which was his fourteenth tragedy, and which he fully intended should be
his last. Many subjects presented themselves
in the scriptures, which he burned to dramatise,
but, fearful of writing too much, he resolved to

pause. By the end of September the whole of.
his tragedies were copied, re-copied, and corrected. In ten months he had versified seven
tragedies, invented, developed, and versified
two, and corrected fourteen. These compositions he had successively read in different com-
panies of both sexes, critical and uncritical.
Alfieri knew the little dependence that could be
placed on the approbation which was lavishly
bestowed on them, and endeavoured to estimate
his success by the involuntary expressions of
the countenances of his auditors, and the interest they evinced in the progress of the story.
The various opinions and criticisms elicited
from his friends, he carefully and scrupu-
lously examined, and endeavoured to profit by
them.

From an author of the ardent and impetuous
character of Alfieri might naturally have been
expected a bold and irregular style of composition, daring flights of imagination, vehement expressions, passion distorted into extravagance,
great beauties, and still greater faults. He ap-

peared formed to trample, with lawless and irrepressible energy, on established rules and opinions, and to have founded a new poetical dy-
nasty on the ruin of the old. Instead of this,
we find him circumscribing himself within
narrower limits than his predecessors, entrench-
ing himself behind the barriers of critical refine-
ment and classical authority, lopping off every
redundancy of sentiment and imagery, restrain-
ing every sally of the fancy, and thinking,
speaking, and writing with the rigidity of a
stoic, and the propriety of a master of the ceremonies. More anxious to render himself in-
vulnerable to the shafts of criticism, than to
seize on the sympathies of the world; to win the
applause of the head, than to command the
homage of the heart; he continued to re-mould,
to condense, and to refine his dramas, till they
acquired the hardness as well as the polish and
durability of marble;—splendid monuments of
art, but cold and cheerless compared to the
varied and glowing creations of nature.

CHAPTER THE THIRTEENTH. 1782-1783.

He commences printing his tragedies—Interruption of his studies—His travels resumed.

REPOSING from his labours, Alfieri remained for some time undecided whether or not he should venture on the desperate course of printing his tragedies. Before he submitted them to the criticism of the public, an opportunity presented itself of trying the effect they were capable of producing, in a less hazardous manner. A select company of amateurs had got up pieces occasionally at a theatre in the palace of the Duke de Grimaldi, the Spanish ambassador. They had hitherto produced only bad translations of French dramas. Alfieri had assisted in the performance of the *Earl of Essex* of T.

G 2

Corneille :· the part of Elizabeth was indifferently played by the Duchess of Zagaralo; but,
as she possessed great beauty and dignity of
person, Alfieri was in hopes, that by advice and
practice she might make a good actress. He
offered one of his own tragedies to these noble
performers, wishing to try the effect of his peculiar style, great simplicity of plot, few characters, and a nervous and abrupt versification,
the opposite of the usual monotonous, antithe-
tical dialogue, on a select and refined audience.
He chose his *Antigone*, the coldest of his plays,
calculating that, if it was favourably received,
his others, which possessed more fire and action,
could not fail of success. His proposition was
eagerly accepted : the Duke and Duchess de
Ceri took the parts of Hæmon and Argia; Antigone, the most important character in the
piece, was supported by the beautiful Duchess
of Zagaralo, and, for want of a better representative, Alfieri himself performed the character
of Creon. Encouraged by the success which
attended this experiment on the taste of the

public, Alfieri determined on submitting his
plays to the dreaded ordeal of the press. As
he found the scruples of the censors at Rome
were vexatious and interminable, he wrote to
his friend, Gandellini, requesting him to get his
tragedies printed at Sienna, a charge which the
latter undertook with enthusiasm. Alfieri wished to risk only four tragedies at first: he sent his
friend the manuscripts, carefully written out, and,
as he thought, sufficiently correct, but when they
appeared in print, he found in them numbern-
less deficiencies in clearness, elegance, and brevity of style. During the two months occupied
in printing them, Alfieri remained at Rome, in
a state of alarm and perplexity; and, but for
shame, would have sent for his manuscripts
back; so much did his horror of public criticism
increase as the day of trial drew near. At
length, the books arrived, correctly but inele-
gantly printed, and the author for several days
was occupied in running from one friend's
house to another, presenting copies of his work,
handsomely bound, to propitiate criticism. He

even solicited for the same purpose an audience
of the Pope, Pius VI. which was readily granted. Alfieri felt very little respect for the Pope
in his pontifical character, and still less as an
individual, as he was neither a man of letters
himself, nor a patron of those who were. He,
however, presented his handsome volume with
due reverence, and his Holiness received the
gift with the most gracious condescension;
opened it, turned over the leaves, and put the
author to the blush with the praises he lavished
on it. He would not permit Alfieri to kiss his
foot, but raised him from the humble posture he
had assumed, tapping him on the cheek with
paternal benignity. The sturdy champion of
liberty was converted in a moment into a devout
courtier; and taking an opportunity when the
Pope, after eulogising the tragic art, asked him
if he had written any other tragedies, he replied,
he had written many, and among others, *Saul*,
the subject of which being taken from the Bible, he wished to dedicate it to his Holiness, if
he would permit him. The Holy Father ex-

cused himself from accepting the proffered honour, saying, he could not allow any theatrical
piece to be inscribed to him. Alfieri was much
mortified at this refusal, and still more, at having
incurred it by his weakness or duplicity. The
reason which induced him to adopt a line of
conduct so foreign to his nature was this.—The
Cardinal York had expressed much dissatisfac-
tion at the frequent visits of the Count to his
sister-in-law, and these ebullitions were reported
by the Priests who surrounded the Cardinal, with
the usual exaggerations. The breach between
them appeared to widen every day, and by pro-
pitiating the Pontiff, Alfieri hoped to secure a
friend in the hour of need against the persecu-
tion he foreboded, and which soon after commenced. The performance of *Antigone*, by gaining him a certain degree of celebrity, had only
made him a more prominent object of curiosity
and scandal.

- In April, 1783, Prince Charles fell dangerously ill, and the Cardinal set off precipitately
for Florence, to see his brother before he died;

but the Prince's malady disappeared as suddenly as it came, and, on his arrival, he found
him out of danger. During his convalescence,
the Priests who came from Rome with the Cardinal united with those who attended the inva-
lid in persuading the former, that he ought no
longer to overlook the conduct of the Countess
under his own roof. The freedoms assumed
by married ladies in Italy are sufficiently notorious, and the Countess had rather kept within
than exceeded the ordinary bounds of propriety,
though the ill-usage she had received from her
husband would have been considered an ample
justification for any deviation from them, in a
country of such easy morality. We have Alfieri's solemn assurance, that their intimacy
never exceeded the bounds of honour; but he
admits, that his attentions were such as to war-
rant the jealousy of the husband and his brother. The Cardinal, on his return to Rome,
intimated to the Countess, that it was absolutely indispensable, that she should put an end
to the assiduities of Count Alfieri, and that nei-

ther his brother nor himself could any longer tolerate them. Not contented with this injunction, the imprudent Cardinal thought fit to proclaim his indignation to the world, raising a clamour throughout the city, and even laying his complaints before the Pope. It was reported, that his Holiness had ordered Alfieri to quit the papal territory, and this rumour, though false, being not improbable, the latter thought it best to be before-hand with his enemies, and to leave Rome before he was compelled. To be absent was less insupportable, than to remain in the same city with the Countess without seeing her: to persist in visiting her publicly was out of the question, and to see her privately might be attended with danger and disgrace. Under these circumstances, he addressed himself to the Sardinian Ambassador, and desired him to inform the Secretary of State, that, aware of the reports in circulation respecting him, and of the scandal they gave rise to, Alfieri valued too highly the peace and reputation of the illustrious lady in question not to put an end to them; that

he had resolved to remove from Rome for some.
time, and he should set out the beginning of
the following month. This spontaneous decla-.
ration was approved of by the Ambassador, and ·
graciously listened to. by the Pope and his Secretary of State. ·   .

'After taking a melancholy. farewell of the
Countess, Alfieri set out from Rome, May 4,
1783. ˙ He proceeded in a state of abstraction·
and insensibility to: surrounding objects, to Sienna, to confide his sorrows to his friend Gandellini. The. latter indulged, instead of vainly
endeavouring to repress the grief of his friend,
and, by his active sympathy, succeeded in soft-
ening his regrets.· All his faculties seemed overwhelmed by this separation from the object of
his affections, and the only exertion he was
capable of, was to write frequent and voluminous letters to the Countess. His literary ambition appeared completely extinguished,· and
even the severe criticisms which were written
on his publication, and which Gandellini occasionally read to him, failed of producing any

irritation. These criticisms were of various
merit and respectability, and the only thing
they agreed in, was to find fault with Alfieri's
style, as harsh, obscure, and unnatural. After
remaining three weeks at Sienna, the fear of
wearying out his friend by his importunate
grief, and his own incapability of study, induced him to seek a change of scene. The Feast
of the Ascension, which he had seen before at
Venice, was about to take place, and he determined to proceed thither. He passed through
Florence in his way, without stopping, unable
to bear the sight of a place where he had spent
so many happy hours. The fatigue and dis-
traction of the journey soon improved his
health, which anxiety and inactivity had visibly
impaired. At Bologna, he quitted the direct
route, to go to Ravenna, to visit the tomb of
Dante, where he spent a whole day in weeping
and meditation. Every day he gave vent to his
feelings in one or more impassioned odes, which
seemed dictated to him by an irresistible impulse. At Venice, when he heard of the ratifi-

cation by England of American independence,
he wrote his Fifth Ode, which terminated his
lyric poem of *America Delivered*. From Venice,
he proceeded to Padua, and did not neglect, as
on a former occasion, to visit the tomb of Petrarch, but devoted a day to meditate and ver-
sify over it. At Padua, he became acquainted
with the celebrated Cesarotti, whose vivacity
and politeness pleased him as much as his writings had done. In his return to Bologna, he
made his fourth poetical pilgrimage to Ferrara,
to visit the tomb and the manuscripts of Ariosto. He had previously seen the mausoleum
of Tasso at Rome, as well as his birth-place at
Sorrento. These two poets, with Dante and
Petrarch, were the gods of his poetical creed,
and he devoutly believed that they comprised
every excellence of style, except the blank
verse of the drama, of which he frequently more
than hints that his own compositions are the
only correct models. Arriving at Milan, he
hastened to join his friend Caluso, in the country, at the château of Masino, near Verceil,

where he remained a few days. Finding himself very near Turin, he was ashamed of leaving its vicinity without visiting his sister: he went thither, accompanied by Caluso, and returned the next morning; having no wish to be publicly seen and recognized in the country he had voluntarily abandoned. He spent a month at Milan, and, during his stay there, had frequent conversations with Parini, the well-known Italian satirist. He consulted him on the structure of dramatic blank verse, but, though he found him intelligent and communicative, yet Parini, as well as Cesarotti, failed to convince Alfieri that they understood the matter half so well as himself. At the beginning of August, he departed for Tuscany by way of Modena and Pistoia. Stopping some days at Florence, he consulted many of the literati of that city respecting his tragedies: he found them very liberal of their advice, which he paid no attention to, and of their censures, which he endeavoured to despise.

On his arrival at Sienna, he committed six

more of his tragedies to the press, and attended
to the printing with so much industry and perseverance, that in two months they were ready
for publication, in spite of the hindrances of
censors and printers. His mind, however, was
so little interested in this operation, that many
faults of style escaped his observation, which
he corrected in subsequent editions. The application and the fatigue of this period brought on
a fit of the gout, which tormented and confined
him to the house for fifteen days, though he obstinately refused to keep his bed. He had experienced an attack of this disorder at Rome,
but his extreme sobriety had prevented it from
being very severe, or of long continuance. He
had just finished printing his tragedies, when
he received from Naples a long and elaborate
critique, by Calsabigi, on his first publication.
As this was much superior in talent, discrimina-
tion, and candour, to any which had appeared,
Alfieri thought fit to answer it. In this reply,
he developed and justified the principles he had
adopted, and the method he had adhered to in

his compositions, and pointed out the miscon-
ceptions of which his critics had been guilty.

The object of all his anxiety, his re-union
with the Countess, being still as uncertain as
ever, he resolved to make a journey into France
and England, not from any desire of re-visiting
those countries, but from a conviction that volition and excitement were necessary to divert
the chagrin which oppressed him. He was also
actuated by a strong desire to purchase as many
English horses as his finances would admit.
His devotion to the Muses had been so much
shaken, that it gave way to his old passion for
horses ; and, metamorphosed from a poet into
a horse-dealer, he set out for London, his imagination engrossed by the forms, sizes, and colours of his future stud. During the eight
months which were occupied in this excursion,
he hardly ever opened a book.

CHAPTER THE FOURTEENTH. 1783-1785.

His horse-dealing expedition to England—His
re-union with the Countess—Resumption of his
literary pursuits.

QUITTING Sienna, with his mind divided between melancholy recollections of his love, and
rapturous anticipations of his horses, he proceeded through Pisa and Lerici to Genoa. His
friend, Gandellini, accompanied him to the latter city, where they stayed a few days. Gandellini returned to Tuscany, and Alfieri embarked for Antibes, where he arrived safely after a
rough passage of forty-eight hours. As soon
as disembarked, he proceeded to Aix, and from
thence to Avignon, where he duly visited the
magic solitude of Vaucluse, consecrated to fame
by the muse of Petrarch, and added his tears

to the fountain of the Sorga. In returning to
Avignon, he composed four sonnets, to commemorate the emotions of the day, which he accounted one of the most happy as well as melancholy of his life. He entered Paris in a fit
of despondence and ennui, and experienced the
same sensations of loathing and disgust at the
filth and finery of this metropolis, as on his first
visit. Though he had letters of introduction to
many of the French literati, the month he spent
at Paris passed away very tediously. The necessity of hearing and speaking their hated language was to him a perpetual source of annoyance and irritation.

Embarking for England in December, he
commenced, as soon as he arrived in London,
to purchase horses: at first, one race-horse; afterwards, three for the saddle; and subsequently, six for a carriage. Of these, he had the
misfortune to lose several before he left England; but for every one that died, he purchased
two; and, at his departure, he increased his
stud to fourteen, the number of his tragedies.

This whimsical numerical coincidence amused
Alfieri, and he was wont to say to himself,
" Thou hast gained a horse by each tragedy,"
alluding to the method of inflicting flagellation
on juvenile delinquents. The composition of
his tragedies appeared to have exhausted his
inventive faculties; the acquisition of his horses
drained his purse. Since the donation of his
property to his sister, he had lived penuriously
for the first three years, and liberally, but fru-
gally, for the other three. - He found himself
master of a considerable sum, produced by the
accumulated interest of his money in the
French funds, which he hitherto had not touch-
ed. The purchase of his fourteen horses, and
the expense of transporting them to Italy, exhausted the greater part of this surplus, and
their support, during five subsequent years,
consumed the remainder. In riding and superintending these horses, and writing letter upon
letter to the Countess, Alfieri spent the time he
resided in London, and thought no more of his
tragedies.

After passing some months in England, he set out on his return, accompanied by his numerous suite of horses and their attendants. The whole of this journey was a series of embarrassments and disasters. Every day some new mischance befell his cavalry, and embittered the pleasure with which he contemplated them. One horse coughed, another became lame, and a third would not eat. In the passage from Dover it was necessary to stow them, like ballast, in the hold of the vessel, till their bright bay colour was not distinguishable through the dirt with which they were covered. On arriving at Calais, they were slung over the sides of the vessel into the sea, as the tide would have prevented a boat from going ashore till the next morning. By unremitting personal exertion, he succeeded in getting his invaluable cargo ashore, without any serious misadventure. The admiration his horses excited at Amiens, Paris, and Lyons, amply repaid him for his cares, and inspired him with courage and perseverance to achieve the remaining and most ha-

H

zardous part of his journey—this was the passage of the Alps, between Lanslebourg and Novalesa. To conduct horses, young and full of spirit, up and down the steep ascents and descents of those mountainous regions, was a task of considerable difficulty and danger. Alfieri took with him to Lanslebourg as many men as he had horses, so that each horse had its conductor, who led him by the bridle. The horses were fastened together by the tail, and to every three was allotted a guide, who, mounted on a mule, superintended and directed their march. In the midst of the convoy was the farrier of Lanslebourg, with the instruments of his profession, ready to lend assistance to any that might require it. Alfieri, as commander-in-chief, brought up the rear, mounted on Frontino, the smallest and lightest of his horses. He had at his side two aides-de-camp, agile and light of foot, whom he despatched with his orders to different parts of the cavalcade. They arrived in this manner, without accident, at the top of Mount Cenis, from which the descent

appeared rather alarming. Alfieri dreaded the
vivacity of his horses, increased by the accele-
rated motion of their descent. He immediately
changed his plan of operations, alighting and
placing himself at their head on foot. To re-
tard their descent, he placed the most heavy
and least spirited of his horses in front, and his
active assistants ran backwards and forwards
from van to rear, to see that they were kept at
a proper distance from each other. The loose
and rough stones over which they passed, caused many of the horses to lose their shoes; but
the arrangement was so complete, that the farrier quickly supplied their wants, and they arrived in safety at Novalesa, without laming
more than one horse.

Alfieri arrived with his convoy at Turin, seven
years after his expatriation, greatly improved in
health by this excursion, but with his learning
and power of application as much deteriorated.
A few days after his arrival, he sent on his
horses, of whose society he began to be wearied, to proceed leisurely to Tuscany, where he in-

tended to rejoin them, and to retrieve the time
and knowledge he lost in his unpoetical pursuits. The pleasure of re-visiting Turin, and
of seeing familiar faces and long-remembered
spots, was chilled by the unkind reception, he
experienced there. His eccentricities, his expatriation, his *penchant* for freedom and for
horses, were causes assigned or understood for
the alienation of almost all his early friends,
who either shunned or received him with mark-
ed and repulsive coldness. He had scarcely
arrived, when his brother-in-law waited on him
to know whether or not he intended to be presented at court. Alfieri, aware that he could
not leave Turin with propriety, without paying
his respects to the King, had made up his mind
to submit to this disagreeable necessity, and
immediately signified his assent. Next morning, he waited on the Minister, to express his
anxiety to be presented to his Majesty, and to
offer him his respectful homage. The Minister
received him very graciously, and expressed the
King's wish to see the Count settled in his own

country, and to avail himself of his services;
that he could not fail to distinguish himself—
and many other *et cæteras*. Alfieri briefly replied, that he was about to return to Tuscany, to
superintend the printing of his works; that he
was at an age when habits were not easily acquired or changed; that he had devoted his life
to literature, and should employ the remainder
of it in the pursuit of literary distinction. The
Minister admitted, that the profession of an author was a good and a fine thing, but observed,
that there were occupations more dignified and
important, of which the Count was every way
worthy. Alfieri thanked him for his good opinion of him, but persisted in his negative. On
being presented to the King, he was received
by his Majesty very graciously, and heard no
more of the employment that had been tendered
him. While at Turin, Alfieri had an opportunity of witnessing the public performance of
his *Virginia* at the Theatre, where, nine years
before, his *Cleopatra* had been brought out.
One of his friends of the Academy, without

being aware of the author's approach, had got it up before his arrival. This gentleman waited on Alfieri to request that he would assist the actors with his instructions, as he had done on the performance of his *Cleopatra;* but the latter, aware of the incapacity of the actors, declined any interference which might implicate him in their failure, though he consented to witness their performance. The Italian tragic actors are in general indifferent, and treated with little respect by the public. Before the time of Alfieri, there were no tragedies which would now draw an audience. Such as they possessed were seldom acted; and for want of better, Metastasio's operas were occasionally performed, with the omission of the airs. The actors, on this occasion, having the Venetian pronunciation, their Italian declamation had all the heaviness and insensibility of a school-boy's recitations. *Virginia*, notwithstanding, was indulgently received, and its repetition was demanded by the audience for the ensuing evening.

After passing some pleasant days with Caluso, whose society seemed to revive his dor-
mant faculties, and to rouse him from his lethar-
gy of idleness, Alfieri left Turin for Asti, to
visit his mother, whom he had only seen once
since he was separated from her in his ninth
year. For this amiable woman, Alfieri always
professed the greatest veneration and love, yet
in a period of twenty-six years, he had visited
her only for a few hours *en passant*. They now
took a mournful farewell of each other, with
the presentiment of never meeting again in this
world.

Once again beyond the Sardinian frontier,
Alfieri seemed to breathe more freely, and to
feel himself finally delivered from the natal
yoke which he had struggled so hard to
shake off. In approaching Modena, the intelligence which he received from the Countess
filled him alternately with grief and hope, and
kept him in a state of the most anxious uncertainty. At Placentia, he received the welcome
information that she was, at length, free, and

was about to quit Rome. After contending
with many difficulties, and making many pecuniary sacrifices to her husband, she obtained
permission, from the Pope and the Cardinal, to
go to the waters of Baden for the benefit of her
health, which was much injured by the restraint
and agitation she had suffered. She set out
from Rome in June, and, travelling along the
shores of the Adriatic, took the road to the
Tyrol, at the same time that Alfieri proceeded
from Turin, through Placentia, Modena, and
Pistoia, to Sienna. The thought of being so
near the Countess, and of being so soon removed to a much greater distance from her, at
once delighted and distracted Alfieri. He
thought of sending on his carriage, and taking
post to rejoin her, but, hesitating and debating
for some time between prudence and passion,
he got the better of his inclination, and proceeded, weeping and exulting, to Sienna and
his friend Gandellini. ..   ,.   .. ...

. So much had his attachment to his horses
estranged him from literary pursuits, that it was

a considerable time before he could force his
mind to any effort of amendment. He, however, managed to finish the third canto of his
Etruria Vindicata, which wanted only a few
stanzas to complete it, and entered upon the
fourth and last canto. This poem was almost
the only one of his compositions which was
written in detached portions and at different
times, without any digested plan. While at
work on this poem, he continued to write and
receive long letters to and from the Countess,
which every day augmented his hopes and his
desire of rejoining her. This impulse soon became so powerful, that he could struggle with
it no longer. Without mentioning his intention
to any one but Gandellini, and feigning to be
bound for Venice, he set out, on the fourth of
August, for Germany. Full of spirits from the
hope of rejoining the Countess, and the reflection that he was traversing the same roads
which she had taken, he proceeded rapidly towards Alsace. The poetic fit was so strong
upon him during this journey, that he made

three or four sonnets every day. He wrote a
poetical epistle to Gandellini, which was his
first and only attempt at burlesque poetry: in
this *jeu d'esprit*, he recommended his favourite
horses to the care of his friend, and gave him
instructions for their treatment. He met the
Countess near Colmar, in Alsace, and in her
society two months glided rapidly away. He
seemed restored at once to the possession of all
his faculties : fifteen days had hardly elapsed
after his arrival, when, as if the presence of his
mistress was his inspiration, he began to compose more tragedies. After writing *Saul*, he
had determined to resign the cothurnus, but he
now found himself impelled to the composition
of his *Agis, Sophonisba*, and *Myrrha*. The two
first, he had often contemplated, but had' hitherto resisted his inclinations to dramatise
them. *Myrrha* was a subject he had considered too revolting for the drama, until, happening
to read in *Ovid's Metamorphoses* the beautiful
and impassioned speech of Myrrha to her nurse,
it had such a powerful effect on his imagination,

that he determined to dramatise the story. The noble play which he has constructed from such hideous and disgusting materials is, perhaps, the most perfect triumph of his genius and skill.

A week after Alfieri's arrival at Colmar, intelligence reached him of the death of the younger brother of Gandellini, and of the dangerous illness of his friend himself: the next post informed him of his death. This was a severe blow to Alfieri, and which he could not have borne with any degree of fortitude, but for the society and sympathy of the Countess, who knew and esteemed Gandellini, and lamented his death as sincerely, though not so violently, as her lover. This melancholy event saddened the short period which remained for them to pass together, and rendered their second separation more bitter. When the dreaded hour of parting arrived, Alfieri tore himself away, and proceeded on his solitary journey, bewildered and overpowered by grief, and weeping incessantly. In this state, he arrived

at Sienna, where the ungovernableness of his
sorrow was augmented by the details of the
sickness and death of his friend, which he eagerly and painfully listened to. He quitted the
house in which Gandellini had lived, and in
which he had himself occupied an apartment,
and could never persuade himself to re-enter it.
Sienna was insupportable without his friend,
and, anxious to escape from scenes which every
moment reminded him of his loss, he set out, in
November, for Pisa. Meantime the Countess,
re-crossing the Alps, had re-entered Italy, and
arrived, in December, at Bologna, where she
stopped to pass the winter, under pretext of the
season being too far advanced for travelling:
thus, without quitting the papal territory, she
avoided returning to her former prison at Rome.
The lovers were thus situated with only the
Apennines between them, yet with the prospect
of being separated for five months. Alfieri received letters from the Countess every three or
four days, but would not venture to visit her,
fearing the scandal of provincial towns, where

any person above the common rank was sure to attract the attention of all the idle and malevolent. He passed the whole of the winter at Pisa, dividing his time between his correspondence with his mistress and the exercise of his horses. In one of his brief intervals of study, he perused the *Letters* of Pliny the younger, which pleased him much by the elegance of the style, and the insight into Roman manners which they afforded him. On perusing Pliny's *Panegyric on Trajan*, he was much surprised and disappointed, recognising in it none of the characteristics of the writer of the *Letters*, and still less of the friend of Tacitus. In a fit of indignant enthusiasm, he seized his pen, and began writing the Panegyric which Pliny *ought* to have written, and which is, perhaps, the most animated and eloquent of the prose compositions of Alfieri. By intense application, the work was completed in five successive mornings, nearly in the same form in which it was afterwards printed. This occupation relieved for a time the anguish of his spirit; and, when

it was finished, he took up the translation he
had made of Sallust ten years before, and applied himself to correct and polish it. The labour of revision possessed too little interest to
divert the current of his reflections, and he soon
laid his Sallust aside to proceed with his *Il
Principe e le Lettere*, of which he had formed
the plan some years before at Florence, and
wrote the first book and two or three chapters
of the second. In the course of the preceding
summer, the third volume of his tragedies had
been printed, and he had sent copies of it to
most of the Italian literati. The presentation
of the work to Cesarotti was accompanied with
a request that he would favour him with his opinion on the style, the composition, and the conduct of his pieces. He received from Cesarotti,
in April, a critical letter on the three tragedies
in this last volume. Alfieri wrote a brief reply
to this letter, thanking Cesarotti for his remarks, and adding notes to some of the observations which he thought admitted of a refuta-
tion. He had intreated Cesarotti to point out

to him proper models for his dramatic blank
verse; and the latter, to his surprise and indignation, instanced his own translations from the
French, *Semiramis*, &c. which Alfieri despised,
considering them as greatly inferior in style to
his own, and unworthy of the translator of Ossian. Alfieri remained at Pisa till the end of
August, employing himself in revising and polishing the first ten tragedies which he had
printed. At the fête which took place in honour of the King and Queen of Naples, who
were on a visit to the Grand Duke Leopold, he
distinguished himself by displaying the unrival--
led beauty and spirit of his English horses. In
spite of the exultation of this triumph, Alfieri
observed with grief and indignation, that in
Italy he could more easily attract attention and
admiration by his horses than his tragedies.

CHAPTER THE FIFTEENTH. 1785-1789.

*He completes his nineteen tragedies—Settles in
Paris—He prints the whole of his works.*

THE Countess had left Bologna, in April, for
France, where most of her friends and relations
resided; and, after remaining at Paris till August, proceeded to Alsace, and took up her
abode in the same house in which she had resided the preceding year. Alfieri set out in
the beginning of September to rejoin. her: he
put all his cavalry in motion, and arrived in Alsace without mischance, taking with him all his
property, except his books, of which he had
left a large portion at Rome. He enjoyed the
society of the Countess for two months only;
at the end of that period, she removed to pass

the winter at Paris, and Alfieri accompanied her as far as Strasburg. This third separation was much less bitter than the preceding ones: the possibility of rejoining her at will, and the prospect of passing the ensuing summer with her, alleviated the pain of parting, and he returned to Alsace in comparative tranquillity, to devote the interval to the Muses. As soon as he was reinstated in his retreat, he began to develope his tragedy of *Agis*, and subsequently *Sophonisba* and *Myrrha*. In January, he finished the second and third books of his *Il Principe e le Lettere*, and a short piece, intended as a tribute to the memory of his friend Gandellini. He, also, conceived and wrote the lyrical part of a drama, on a plan entirely new, which he called a *melo-tragedy*, and in which his object was to unite the attraction of music with the grandeur and pathos of tragedy. The subject was the *Death of Abel*; angels and demons form part of the dramatis personæ, and are the singers of the play: Adam and Eve, and their two sons, discourse in blank verse and without music. He now finished the fourth canto of his *Etruria Vindicata*, and polished and endeavoured to make it amalgamate with the three preceding cantos, which he had written by snatches during a period of ten years, and which did not harmonise throughout so completely as his other pieces. The Countess, in one of her letters from Paris, happened to mention her having been present at the performance of Voltaire's *Brutus*. A tragedy on *Brutus* by a Frenchman and a plebeian, and one who styled himself " gentleman in ordinary to the King," provoked the spleen of the poetical aristocrat, and he determined to show what a patrician could produce on such a subject. He immediately conceived the plots of his two *Brutuses*, such as he afterwards developed. The *twelve* tragedies to which Alfieri had restricted himself now amounted to *nineteen*, and, on the last, he renewed his vow to Apollo, that he would not increase that number. For five or six successive months, he devoted himself to literature with unremitting diligence. On ri-

sing in the morning, he began to write five or
six long pages to the Countess; then applied
himself to study or composition until two or
three in the afternoon, and afterwards mounted
his horse and rode for a couple of hours. Such
close application brought on a violent attack of
the gout, which, for the first time, confined him
to his bed, where he remained suffering and im-
moveable for fifteen days. This malady probably saved him from the ill effects of a system
of extreme mental exertion, which his mind
might have sunk under but for this unwelcome
interruption. By repose and a strict regimen,
he was nearly recovered by the end of May.
Accidental circumstances preventing the return
of the Countess to the country at the appointed
time, he sunk into a profound melancholy,
which, for the space of three months, incapaci-
tated him for effectual exertion. The arrival of
the Countess, at the end of August, restored
him to mental and bodily health. He returned
to his labours with fresh vigour, and, by the
end of the year, completed the versification of

his *Agis, Sophonisba,* and *Myrrha;* developed his
two *Brutuses,* and wrote his first *Satire.* The
latter species of composition, he had attempted
at Florence nine years before, but had abandon-
ed.it, owing to his unskilfulness in the Italian
language and versification. Before he quitted
Alsace, he went over and examined all his poems, of which he had already revised and polished the greater part. After an uninterrupted
residence of fourteen months in the country, he
set out, with the Countess, for Paris. Uncertain how long he might remain there, he left his
favourite horses in Alsace, and took with him
only his manuscripts and a few of his books.
The noise and offensive odour of the French
capital so grievously annoyed Alfieri after his
domestication in the country, that had he been
alone he would not have remained a day in it;
but the company of the Countess reconciled
him to every personal inconvenience, and converted this purgatory into a paradise. He endeavoured to turn his stay in Paris to some account in his literary pursuits, but he found the

French *savans* very superficially acquainted
with the Italian language and literature, and
could not hope to derive any assistance from
them on that subject. On the dramatic art they
were willing to harangue for ever, but Alfieri
had no great respect for their dicta, and contented himself with listening in silence, as he
had no relish for contradictory discussion. He
had finished versifying *The First Brutus,* and,
by a whimsical sally, obliged himself to recast
his *Sophonisba* entirely. He happened to read
this piece to a Frenchman whom he had known
at Turin, and who had given him some judicious
advice on the composition of his *Philip,* which
he had read to him in French prose. The
Frenchman listened to him with mute attention; but Alfieri, who kept a watchful eye on
his companion, did not perceive that anxiety
expressed in his countenance which he expected to excite; and feeling convinced, by the
time he got into the third act, that the interest
grew colder and colder, by an irresistible impulse, he tossed the tragedy into the fire. The

Frenchman started up, surprised at this sally, and endeavoured to rescue the manuscript from its fate; but the infuriate author, seizing the tongs, thrust his unfortunate offspring into the middle of the fire, and kept it there till it was entirely consumed. Some months after this sacrifice, he happened to take up the original sketch, and finding in it something that pleased him, in spite of the original defects of the story, he versified it again, abridging and altering it considerably from his first design. He embraced the opportunity which his residence in Paris afforded of re-printing the whole of his tragedies in a handsome and correct edition. In order to judge of the accuracy and beauty of Parisian typography, he committed to the press his *Panegyric on Trajan,* which, being short, was finished in a month. The manner in which it was executed induced him to change his printer, and to enter into an engagement with Didot the Elder, who, besides being well-informed and devoted to his art, was perfectly conversant in the Italian language. The first volume of the tra-

gedies went to press in May, but the progress of
the work was considerably retarded by the departure of Alfieri to Alsace in the following month,
though arrangements were made to forward the
proofs to him every week. Many errors of style,
which had escaped him in the former edition,
became visible in the revision of the sheets, and
added greatly to the labour and delay of correction. The love of tranquillity and the country,
the uninterrupted society of the Countess, the
enjoyment of his much loved books, and his
more loved horses, were strong incentives to
this return to his seclusion in Alsace. A few
weeks after their arrival in the country, Alfieri
and the Countess set out to meet Caluso, who
had promised to pass the summer with them, at
Geneva, and returned with him through Switzerland. The first discourse which Caluso had
with Alfieri, to the great surprise of the latter,
turned upon matrimony. Caluso had received
from Alfieri's anxious mother a commission,
somewhat strange, when her son's age, habits,
pursuits, and connexion were considered :—it

was a proposal of marriage with a rich heiress,
the daughter of one of his father's friends.
Who the lady was, Alfieri had not the curiosity
to ask, or even to guess : he rejected the offer,
as it was made, laughing; and they arranged an
answer between them to satisfy the old lady.
This affair being settled, Alfieri enjoyed for
some time in his friend's society the pleasure of
conversing in pure Tuscan, and of discussing his
literary views with a congenial spirit. Their
happiness was interrupted by the illness of
Alfieri, who was attacked by a violent dysentery,
which reduced him to the last extremity. Des-
pairing of recovery, his greatest affliction was
the thought of leaving his works without his
finishing touches, and Caluso, at his entreaty,
promised to take charge of them and of his post-
humous reputation. After the fifteenth day his
disorder took a favourable turn, and gradually
left him by the thirtieth. In six weeks he was
cured, but reduced to a skeleton; and so en-
feebled, that for fourteen weeks he could not
move without assistance. He remained so weak

that he was unequal to the task of revising his
works ; and the first three tragedies which passed through the press did not receive the tenth
part of the correction he intended to bestow on
them. This circumstance was his principal reason for re-printing them afresh three years
after. When his friend was somewhat recovered, Caluso, being obliged by his literary avocations to return to Turin, where he was Secretary
to the Academy of Sciences, wished, before
going to Italy, to visit Strasburg. Though
Alfieri was still weak, he resolved to accompany
him to this city, that he might prolong the pleasure of his company. They set out, in October, accompanied by the Countess, and in this
excursion they visited the magnificent printing-
press, furnished with the types of Baskerville,
which M. de Beaumarchais had established at
Kehl, for the purpose of printing an edition of
the works of Voltaire. The accuracy of the
workmen and the beauty of the type, as well as
the knowledge he possessed of M. de Beaumarchais, rendered Alfieri desirous of printing, at

I

this establishment, the whole of his miscellaneous works, which might have experienced some
obstruction from the vigilance and severity of
the French censorship. Having obtained permission from Beaumarchais to make use of his
presses, he left his five Odes on American Independence to be printed as a specimen. Being
perfectly satisfied with the correctness and
beauty of the impression, he had the remainder
of his works printed in the same manner, in the
course of the two following years. A proof was
forwarded to him, at Paris, every week, and he
was sure to make abundance of alterations in it.
He was delighted with the care and docility of
the printers at Kehl, contrasted with Didot's,
who exhausted his patience and drained his
purse by their exorbitant charges for corrections. From Strasburg, the party returned to
Colmar, and a few days after, Caluso left them
for Turin. Alfieri and the Countess remained
in the country till the middle of December;
when they set off for Paris. Previous to his removal, he had versified his *Second Brutus*, the

last of his tragedies. As his arrangements were
likely to detain him at Paris for a considerable
time, his first care, on arriving, was to look out
for a house, and he had the good fortune to find
one, very cheerful and very tranquil, in the
Fauxbourg St. Germain. The situation was
fine and airy, and the prospect picturesque; and
he could enjoy the seclusion of the country, as
at the Baths of Dioclesian. He brought all his
horses with him, though not without some difficulty: of these, he presented one half to the
Countess, who continued to have a separate
establishment, and was thus lightened of much
trouble and expense. As soon as he was settled,
he devoted himself to the harassing and laborious task of superintending the press. In February, 1788, the Countess received intelligence
of the death of her husband, at Rome. She was
greatly afflicted on hearing of this event, though
his dissolution had been expected for some time,
and though she was finally delivered from her
tyrant and left mistress of herself. The only

obstacle to the legal union of Alfieri and the
Countess was now removed; but it remains more
than doubtful whether they were ever married.
If they were married, they both took as much
pains to conceal the circumstance as is usually
taken to make it public; yet it is-difficult to
assign any adequate reason for a concealment
so injurious to 'the reputation of the lady.*

Early in the year 1789, Alfieri had completed
both his publications: the six volumes of tragedies printed at Paris, and the miscellaneous
pieces at Kehl. He had his *Panegyric on Trajan* re-printed with many corrections; adding
an Ode on the taking of the Bastille, and an
apologue on existing circumstances, in which
the English were represented -as the *bees*, and

---

* On the tomb of Alfieri, we are told, that Louisa, Countess of
Albany, was his *only love*, " quam unice dilexit." A church was
not the place to boast of an illicit attachment; but the silence of
Caluso, who wrote the epitaph, respecting any legal connection
between them, naturally leads to the inference, that he knew, but
did not choose to tell, that his friend was never married to the widow of the Pretender.

the French as the *flies,* of the fable. He had
now nothing remaining unprinted, except his
melo-tragedy of *Abel,* and his translation of
Sallust.

CHAPTER THE SIXTEENTH.   1789-1792.

The French Revolution—Alfieri's fourth visit to
England—An unexpected recognition—Flight
of Alfieri and the Countess from Paris.

DURING the latter part of the period occupied
in printing, Alfieri lived in a fever of anxiety
and rage. The daily disturbances from the commencement of the convocation of the States-
General threatened a termination to his publications, and, after so much fatigue and so many
expenses, he saw himself in danger of a ship-
wreck within sight of port.   Didot's men were
metamorphosed into politicians, and wasted
whole days in reading newspapers, instead of
composing and correcting.   Alfieri was almost
distracted; but, at length, to his great joy, the

tragedies were finished, and were forwarded to
Italy and other parts of the continent, from
whence he, in due time, received intelligence,
that the works had sold well and met with general approbation.

Alfieri, in common with wiser men and better
politicians than himself, had hailed, with joy, the
first dawn of French emancipation, and had written an ode to celebrate the taking of the Bastille.* But a revolution, which uprooted the power of the aristocracy as well as the kingly authority, was utterly at variance with the patrician
feelings of the haughty Piedmontese. His fancied love of freedom resulted from a hatred of
the few whom fortune had placed above him, and
not from any sympathy with the thousands who
were beneath him: chance might have made
him a patriot, but nature intended him for a tyrant. He would not have abolished despotism,
but divided it among a privileged class. From
the visionary zealot of freedom, who had spurn-

* As well as some other pieces, of the same tendency, which
he afterwards thought proper to disclaim.

ed the mild authority of his native sovereign,
might have been expected an ardent and honest
sympathy in the struggles of a great nation for
deliverance, and a lenient feeling even for their
errors and excesses; but, before the revolution
had assumed its wilder and more sanguinary
character, Alfieri became as furious in his hatred of Gallic innovation, as the most bigoted
supporter of the old *regime.* His own turbulent
feelings had taught him that a Count ought to
be free; but he had yet to learn, that a plebeian
had any claim to the same privilege. He beheld, with abhorrence, the encroachments of the
people, and his hatred of kingly authority gave
way to his horror of the usurpation of the mob.
His personal dislike of the French made him
look on their proceedings with a jaundiced eye,
and he could never forgive them for being free
while Italy remained enslaved. He became
ashamed of having ever felt and thought in
common with the "tiger-monkeys," as he called them; and his subsequent writings breathe
a furious and indiscriminating spirit of hostili-

ty, which reflects little credit on the judgment
or feelings of the author. The dread of appearing to countenance the revolutionary dema-
gogues induced him to delay the publication of
the works which he had printed at Kehl, with
the exceptions of *America Delivered* and *Departed Virtue*. Melancholy presentiments of
the future, the state of inaction in which he
was left by the completion of his printing, with
the consciousness of having produced, in his
fourteen years' labour, something capable of
immortality, induced him to write his *Memoirs*,
which he terminated at Paris, the 27th of May,
1790, in his forty-second year, intending not to
resume his narrative till his sixtieth, when, if he
lived so long, he calculated on terminating his
literary career. This task being accomplished,
after a short interval of restless idleness, he determined to amuse himself by translating some
parts of the *Æneid*, distrusting his present com-
petence to the task of invention and originality.
At first, he translated only such passages as
particularly pleased him, but, finding his em-

I 2

ployment both useful and agreeable, he began
to translate it regularly. To diversify his labour, without interrupting his intimacy with the
Latin, he commenced a version of Terence, intending, by the study of so pure a model, to
qualify himself for writing comedies, and to
form an appropriate and peculiar style. He
proceeded regularly with his version of Virgil
and Terence on alternate days, and, by the end
of April, 1791, when he left Paris, he had translated the four first books of the Æneid, and The
Andrian, The Eunuch, and The Self-tormentor of
Terence. His faculty of original composition
appeared extinct, and six melo-tragedies, which
he had intended to compose, were given up in
despair. During this and the two following
years, he composed only some epigrams, to give
vent to his hatred of democratic tyranny. He
attempted a sort of melo-drama, entitled Count
Ugolino, but incapacity or apathy prevented its
developement. In the latter end of 1790, he
made a short tour with the Countess into Nor-
mandy; and, anxious to obtain another respite

from the horrors which surrounded them, they
set out, in the spring of the following year, for
England. As they intended to remain there
for some time, they took their horses with
them, and disposed of their house at Paris.
The Countess had never visited England before,
and was highly delighted with it in some respects, but as little in others. Though it presented nothing new to Alfieri, he admired it
still on account of the government, of which
he, more than ever, appreciated the excellence;
but the climate and the late hours of English
society were equally destructive to his spirits
and his health. He was speedily attacked by
the flying gout, which he thought a disorder in-
digenous in the island; and the charm of novelty being dissipated, the Countess, as well as
himself, began to get weary of England.

The political horizon in France became more
gloomy and threatening. About this time, the
unfortunate Louis made his escape from Paris;
but, being re-taken at Varennes, was brought
back to the capital, and confined more rigor-

ously than ever. Alfieri and the Countess experienced considerable embarrassment in their finances. They both derived three-fourths of their incomes from France, where the currency had disappeared, and was replaced by an excessive issue of paper money, which was falling every day in value. Deprived, in a great measure, of the means of subsisting out of France, they submitted to the frightful necessity of returning thither, as the only place where they could live on this depreciated paper. After making a short excursion, in August, to Bath, Bristol, and Oxford, they returned to London, and from thence proceeded to Dover, where they embarked a few days after.

In his third visit to England in 1783, Alfieri had neither seen, nor had he endeavoured to learn any thing of Lady L——. Public report had apprised him, that, soon after her divorce, her husband had died, and that she had married again with some obscure individual. During the four months he had just passed in England, he had never heard her name mentioned, and was ignorant if she still lived. On embarking at Dover, Alfieri went to the vessel a short time before the Countess, in order to see that every thing was in readiness. Just as he was on the point of entering it, he happened to cast a look towards a number of persons who were assembled on the shore, and the first object that met his eyes was the *ci-devant* Lady L——: still handsome, and scarcely altered from what she had been twenty years before. As he gazed more intently, a gracious smile of recognition convinced him that he was not mistaken. Bewildered with the multitude of conflicting emotions which her appearance conjured up, he threw himself into the packet-boat, and did not again go on shore. In a few minutes, the Countess arrived, and they weighed anchor. Alfieri acquainted the Countess, between whom and himself a reciprocal frankness and confidence had always existed, of his unexpected interview with Lady L——. The Countess informed him, that some ladies, who had accompanied her to the vessel, had pointed out her

ladyship to her, and had related some of the in-
cidents of her past and present life. On arriving at Calais, he could not be satisfied, without
writing to the lady; for whom he had once experienced so extravagant a passion, and whom
accident had so oddly brought again in his way.
He despatched a letter to a banker, at Dover,
to be forwarded to Lady L——, directing the
answer to be forwarded to him at Brussels. In
his letter, he expressed the strong emotions
which her re-appearance had excited, and the
remorse which he felt at having been the cause
of her degradation from her former rank to an
obscure and ignoble life, when, but for the no-
toriety and scandal of his attachment, she might
have retrieved her first false step. A month
after, he received her reply, expressing herself
contented and happy in her present situation,
and grateful for having been withdrawn from a
rank for which she did not feel herself formed:
that her life glided away pleasantly in the less
polished and more sincere society in which she
was now placed, and in the amusements of

drawing, reading, and music: that, above all, she was happy in the unalterable affection of a brother, whom she loved beyond the world. She concluded, by expressing the pleasure she had felt at hearing the name of Count Alfieri mentioned at Paris and London, with applause, as an eminent writer—and her wishes for his continued happiness, as well as that of the amiable Princess with whom he travelled, and to whom she heard he was tenderly attached.

Before returning to their prison at Paris, Alfieri and his companion made a tour in Holland, proceeding along the coast from Calais to Bruges and Ostend, and from thence through Antwerp and Rotterdam to Amsterdam and the Hague. By the end of November, they arrived at Brussels, and passed some weeks in that city with the mother and sister of the Countess. On their return to Paris, they hired a handsome and commodious house, and awaited patiently, but anxiously, for a more fortunate order of events. Two years before, Alfieri had sent for all the books which he had left at Rome in

1783, and which, added to those he had purchased in England and Holland, formed a considerable collection. · He divided his time between his library and the society of the Countess, and endeavoured to shut his eyes and ears
to the tumult and confusion around him. During the whole of his last abode at Paris, he
studiously kept aloof from political discussion,
and the society of the sanguinary factions
which successively predominated. In March,
he received letters from his mother, expressing
her inquietude at his remaining in a country so
disturbed, where the exercise of the Catholic
religion was no longer allowed, and where only
new calamities could be expected. Before her
son's return to Italy, she breathed her last, having just completed her seventieth year. The
Revolutionists were now endeavouring to abo-
lish the only remaining vestige of royalty—the
name: the famous tenth of August speedily
followed with all its horrors. After this catas-
trophe, Alfieri thought only of withdrawing the
Countess from the dangers which surrounded

them. He would not defer for a moment the preparations for their departure, and, by the twelfth, they were ready for their journey. To obtain leave to quit Paris and the kingdom, at this time, was attended with great difficulty; but, by unremitting exertions, he procured passports on the fifteenth for them as foreigners; his own from the Venetian envoy, and one for the Countess from the Danish ambassador, the only ministers who had not quitted the miserable court of Louis XVI. He had still greater difficulty in obtaining passports from the section of Mont Blanc, in which they resided. It was necessary to have a passport for each individual, whether master or servant, describing their sex, age, size, the colour of their hair and eyes, &c. Furnished with these documents, they fixed their departure for the twentieth, but a well-founded presentiment of danger induced them to set off on the afternoon of the eighteenth. Arriving at the Barriere Blanche, the nearest outlet to the Calais road which they intended to take, they found there an officer and three or

four of the National Guard, who, after examining their passports, prepared to open the barrier,
when a croud of thirty or forty individuals, of
the lowest description, sallied out of a neigh-
bouring cabaret, half-naked and frantic with in-
toxication. As soon as these wretches saw the
two carriages of the fugitives, laden with trunks
and other property, they began to vociferate,
that, if all the rich people were thus allowed to
leave Paris with their wealth, they should all be
reduced to want and beggary. A dispute immediately ensued between the few guards and the
mob, the former attempting to clear a passage for
the travellers, and the latter to detain them forcibly. Alfieri leaped out of the carriage into the
midst of the crowd, armed with his seven passports, and began to storm and out-clamour the
rabble, knowing, by experience, that this was the
only way to deal with Frenchmen. The passports
were read one after another, by such of the
party as could read. Furious and half mad
with the delay, Alfieri forgot or despised the
danger which menaced them. He snatched his

passport out of their hands, vociferating, "See—
hear—my name is Alfieri—I am an Italian, not
a Frenchman—tall, meagre, pale, and red-
haired.—Look at me—see if I am not the individual described. I have a passport—it is correct—it is given by the proper authorities—I
want to pass—and by G—— I will pass." This
tumult lasted near half an hour, and the crowd
continued to increase round the travellers.
Some cried out to burn the carriages, some to
stone the party, but the greater number insisted
that they were some of the *noblesse* flying with
their wealth, and that they should be taken to
the Hotel de Ville, to be delivered up to justice.
At length the assistance of the guards, who occasionally threw in a word in their favour, and
the stentorian clamour of Alfieri, bore down
the opposition of the mob—the guards made
signs to him to remount the carriage—the
postilions sprung on their horses—and the party
dashed through the barrier at full gallop, pursued
by the hisses and curses of the disappointed
ruffians. In two days and a half they arrived at

Calais. The Municipal Officers, who examined
their passports on the road, were ignorant of the
recent events at Paris, and were horror-struck on
perceiving the name of the King, which had
been printed on them, erased. The party found
no difficulty in pursuing their journey, by
Gravelines, to the frontiers of Flanders. They
learned afterwards that they were the first
foreigners who had escaped out of Paris and
the kingdom after the fatal tenth of August.
The health of the Countess requiring some repose after the anxiety and alarm she had suffered,
they remained a month with her relations at
Brussels. Alfieri received letters from the domestics whom he had left at Paris, informing
him that on the day *intended* for his departure
(but which he had luckily forestalled) orders
had been issued to arrest the Countess, whose
rank and wealth were crimes sufficient to have
condemned her before a Parisian tribunal.
Finding their victims had escaped, they declared
them emigrants, confiscated their horses, furni-
ture, and books, and sequestrated their revenues.

Alfieri and his fair friend were too grateful for having escaped the horrors of the second of September, which occurred so speedily after their ·flight, to repine at this deprivation of fortune, and comforted themselves with the reflection of having saved their lives, and the means of supporting them.

CHAPTER THE SEVENTEENTH.   1792-1800.

*He returns to Florence—His Anti-gallican compo-
sitions—Learns Greek in his forty-sixth year—
His translations from that language—Invasion
of Italy by the French.*

SETTING off for Italy on the first of October,
they passed through Aix-la-Chapelle, Frankfort,
Augsburg, and Inspruck; crossed the Alps, and
arrived at Florence on the third of November.
Alfieri was overjoyed in finding himself again in
the Tuscan territory, and at hearing his favourite dialect spoken, and never after quitted
the country of his adoption.   Though they had
both lost the greater part of their property, they
had still enough left to live with comfort and
respectability.   The satisfaction of finding his
tragedies a subject of conversation, and of seeing

them frequently, though indifferently performed,
roused his literary ardour, which had so long
slumbered. His first production, after three
years of inaction, was an apology for Louis XVI.
He re-commenced his translations of Terence
and the *Æneid*, which he completed in the ensuing year, and re-copied and re-touched his
translation of Sallust. He also wrote a short
historical and satirical view of the French Revolution, as an introduction to a collection of
Sonnets, Epigrams, and other short pieces, on
the melancholy events in France, which he entitled *Misogallo*. This work, of which he speaks
with great complacency in his *Memoirs*, is below
mediocrity, and betrays all the rage of impotent
scurrility. The Epigrams are seasoned with
more malice than wit, and would be considered
wretched, even as the production of a middling
author. The *Misogallo* however contains two
pieces well worthy of perusal : the defence
which Alfieri would have put into the mouth of
Louis in the Convention, and the apology of the author for his detestation of the French Revolution.

Of his large library, he had only preserved about a hundred and fifty small volumes of the classics, which he continued to study assidu-ously. He had not courage to attempt the completion of the melo-tragedies he had so long meditated. The drudgery to which he had subjected himself, during the five years oc-cupied by the impression of his works, and the cares and disappointments he had experienced, had deprived him of that warmth and energy which he deemed essential to such composi-tions. His splenetic feelings prompted him to resume his satires, but, after completing the se-cond and part of the third, his attention was diverted by a whim for performing in his own tragedies. Among his juvenile acquaintance at Florence, there were some who possessed much taste and some talent for the histrionic art. They performed *Saul* in a private house to a select audience, and with great success. At the end of 1793, he removed to a small but com-modious house on the Arno, near the bridge of Santa Trinita, of which he kept possession for

the remainder of his life. The convenience,
the airiness, and the delightful situation of his
new dwelling had a beneficial effect on his
health and spirits. A great portion of his time
and attention, during 1794 and the following
year, was devoted to his theatrical performances. His principal characters were Saul, Ju-
nius Brutus, Don Carlos, and Philip, which he
performed with increasing spirit and success,
and his co-adjutors under his care promised to
become, if not a good, yet the best tragic company in Italy, had his patience, health, and
finances been adequate to their continued guidance. His last performance was at Pisa, where
he had been invited by a company of amateurs,
during the Feast of the Illumination: the character was his favourite one of Saul.

Since his return to Tuscany, he had re-pur-
chased many books, particularly the best Italian
authors, to which he added many of the Latin
classics, and the Græco-Latin editions of the
Greek classics. At the age of forty-six, he felt
ashamed of having remained ignorant of the

K

Greek language, and of having been twenty
years a dramatic and lyric poet, yet not being
able to read the tragic writers of Greece, nor
Homer, nor Pindar, in their own language. He
spent nearly a year and half in perusing attentively the Latin translations of the best Greek
writers. In this period, he wrote occasional
poems, and increased the number of his satires
to seven. In 1796, the invasion of Italy by the
French took place; an event which Alfieri contemplated with alarm and horror. Too haughty
and inflexible to bend to the storm, or to fall
in with the prevailing party, he endeavoured to
shut himself out from the world, and prosecu-
ted his studies with more intense application.
After hovering for some time on the confines of
the Greek language, he determined on making
himself master of it, and set about the task
with characteristic impetuosity and devotedness. He had never possessed any aptitude for
the acquirement of language, and he was now
at a time of life when the memory becomes less
susceptible and tenacious. He had never mas-

tered the English language, though he had
made several attempts, and had mixed so much
in English society. He had a great aversion to
the study of grammar, and was imperfectly acquainted even with his own.—The Greek characters disgusted him, and, for a long time, he
was unable to retain their forms in his memory.
His invincible perseverance, however, surmount-
ed every obstacle, and, without instructor or assistance of any kind, he made himself, by the
end of 1797, sufficiently master of the language,
to read most of the Greek writers with facility.
His intense application strengthened instead of
weakening his faculties as he had apprehended.
In the course of this year, he composed ten
more satires, and revised a great portion of his
poems. Becoming more enamoured as he became more intimately acquainted with the
Greek, he translated the *Alceste* of Euripides;
afterwards, the *Philoctetes* of Sophocles and the
Persians of Æschylus; and, when more completely conversant with the language, the *Frogs*
of Aristophanes. He was assisted in these

translations by a young man of talent and respectability, and the manner in which his assistance was received is singular and characteristic. The tutor slowly read aloud the Greek original, translating it as he went on, and Alfieri walked about the room with his pencil and tablets, noting down his version. When his assistant recited too rapidly, or when he did not fully understand the passage, he held up his pencil, and the last sentence was slowly repeated, or the reading stopped until a tap of the pencil on the table warned the translator to proceed. The lesson began and concluded with a silent obeisance, and, during twelve months of instruction, the Count scarcely uttered as many words to his preceptor. The latter hinted a remonstrance to the Countess on this coldness and reserve, but she assured him, that the Count had the highest esteem for him and his services.

When Alfieri first read the *Alceste* of Euripides, he was so much pleased and affected, that, in spite of his oath, he felt irresistibly impelled to form the plan of a tragedy on the same sub-

ject. This done, he continued to prosecute his
studies for two years without proceeding with
his tragedy, when the perusal of the Greek original heated his imagination so much, that he
could no longer restrain his inclination to develope it. He composed, without a pause, the
whole of the first act, and inscribed on the mar-
gin, " Written in a paroxysm of enthusiasm,
and while shedding tears." He wrote the remaining four acts, sketched the choruses, and
composed a preface to the tragedy, but without
any intention of versifying it. However, in the
latter end of 1798, the re-perusal of the original
induced him to complete it, but, fearing to in-
cur the charge of ingratitude or plagiarism, he
placed this piece among his translations, by the
title of *The Second Alceste*, in contradistinction
to his version of the *Alceste* of Euripides. The
Alceste is the happiest of his latter efforts, and
possesses a tender pathos which Alfieri could
not or would not infuse into his other tragedies,
in which he aimed at a stoical elevation of sentiment. Alfieri had kept his study of Greek a

profound secret, even. from Caluso. Sending
his portrait, painted by Fabre, to his sister, he
wrote on the back of the canvas two Greek
verses from Pindar. His sister was delighted
with the picture, and observing the inscription
at the back, sent for Caluso to decipher it.
The Abbé was surprised to find a scrap of
Greek attached to the portrait, and, convinced
that his friend was incapable of the paltry pe-
dantry of making use of a quotation which he
did not understand, he wrote immediately to
task him with his secresy. Alfieri sent him, in
reply, a letter in Greek, adding some specimens
of his translations. The praises which the Abbé
bestowed upon his proficiency, incited him to
follow the study of the Greek with unabated
ardour.

The speedy occupation of Tuscany by the ar-
mies of the Republic now appeared inevitable.
In November, 1798, the French troops entered
Lucca, and threatened Florence. Alfieri anticipated their arrival with gloomy resolution. Having always proclaimed his unmingled hatred

of the French democracy and its adherents, he
expected to experience every species of outrage
from them. He determined not to court their
resentment causelessly, but, if called upon, to
perish with the dignity and firmness becoming
an admirer of Roman virtue. Anxious lest what
he left behind him might lower his literary reputation, he set to work, examining, revising,
and polishing his unpublished pieces, and in de-
stroying what appeared unfit for the public eye.
Having accomplished his fiftieth year, he seri-
ously bade farewell to the Muses. His last
poem was a pindaric ode, which he entitled
Teleutodia: he wrote, indeed, a few sonnets
subsequently, but these he took no care to preserve. He thought it better to lay aside the
lyre while in the full possession of his faculties,
than to wait till age or imbecility compelled him
to resign it. His *Misogallo* was not yet sufficiently finished for publication, nor would it have
been very prudent to have sent it forth to the
world at this conjuncture: to secure this favourite but imbecile composition from the possibi-

lity of destruction, he caused ten copies of it
to be made, which he deposited in different
places.

Having thus " set his house in order," he felt
tranquil, and prepared for the worst fortune
that could befall him. To employ his time to
the best advantage, he adopted a regular rou-
tine of study, to which he rigidly adhered.
Monday and Tuesday, he devoted to the perusal
and study of the Scriptures: Wednesday and
Thursday, to Homer: Friday, Saturday, and
Sunday, (during the first year) to Pindar, the
most difficult of the Greek poets. The Bible he
perused first in the Septuagint version, afterwards in Diodati's Italian translation, and lastly
in the Latin Vulgate. Homer he read in the
original, pronouncing every word aloud, and
rendering literally into Latin an immense number of verses for reconsideration and study. He
also perused attentively the Greek Scholiast and
the Latin notes of Barnes, Clarke, and Ernestus.
By the most patient and persevering labour, having made himself master of the lyric flights of

Pindar, he applied himself to study and analyse
Sophocles and Æschylus with equal industry.
Having arranged this course of study, he sent
away all the books which he did not absolutely
want to a house which he had taken in the country, that his library might not again fall a prey
to the rapacity of the French. The Republican
army entered Florence on the twenty-fifth of
March, 1799, and, on the same day, Alfieri quitted the city, and retired with the Countess to
his house in the country, removing all their property, and abandoning their mansion to the occupation of the military. He remained in the
country with very few domestics, and without
any society but that of the Countess. The latter was well acquainted with the English, Ger-
man, French, and Italian languages, and was
perfectly conversant with their literature, as
well as with the best translations of the classics. Her taste and acquirements enabled her
to discuss with Alfieri his plans and pursuits;
and the society of this amiable and accomplished female was his best and only refuge from the

tedium of study, and the agitations of his own
wounded spirit. She was, indeed, the only link
which united him to the world : without her, he
would have degenerated into a savage, or have
railed himself into a madman.

In this period of terror, distrust and appre-
hension kept friends and acquaintances aloof.
The liberty which existed in France had been
proclaimed in Florence, and the system of military despotism was in active operation. Arbitrary arrests in the night were of frequent oc-
currence, and young men, of the first families,
were torn from the arms of their friends, and
carried off as hostages. This state of things
lasted till the fifth of July, when the victories
of the Allies obliged the French to evacuate
Tuscany. A month after this welcome event
had taken place, Alfieri returned to Florence;
but he was scarcely settled in his old habita-
tion, when his equanimity received a shock
which he had long expected and dreaded.
There fell into his hands an advertisement of
Molini, an Italian bookseller at Paris, announc-

ing a complete edition of the works of Alfieri,
both in prose and verse, and adding the titles
of the different pieces : among these, Alfieri recognised, with dismay, all the works which he
had printed at Kehl, but never published. After his escape from France, being apprehensive
that the faction which confiscated his library
would not let his unpublished works escape
their rapacity, he had inserted a notice in all
the Italian gazettes, disclaiming any publication
that might bear his name, unless published by
himself. The sentiments which he had formerly
maintained were so little in unison with his
present feelings, and he felt so much ashamed
and exasperated at having ever coincided with
a set of ruffians whom he hated and despised,
that his first impulse was to issue a counter-ad-
vertisement, detailing the manner in which he
had been robbed, and to publish his *Misogallo*
as an antidote to his former, and a vindication
of his present politics. But a regard for the
safety of those connected with him prevented
this step, and he contented himself with repeat-

ing his former advertisement, and adding, by
way of postscript, that having heard that what
was called a complete edition of his works was
about to be published at Paris, he renewed the
protest which he had made six years before.
Alfieri was at a loss to conjecture why a new
edition was printed in preference to publishing
that which he had printed at Kehl, and of which
the type and paper were superb. Five hundred
copies of the book had been left at Paris, in
bales on which he had written *Italian tragedies*,
a title which probably condemned them to destruction as waste paper.

CHAPTER THE EIGHTEENTH. 1800-1803.

*Alfieri and the French General—Manners and
habits of Alfieri in his latter years—His six
Comedies—He institutes the Order of Homer
—Death of Alfieri.*

IN October, 1800, the French re-entered Tuscany, and took possession of Florence: this ir-
ruption was so sudden and unexpected, that
Alfieri had not time to escape into the country
before the arrival of the enemy. He had obtained, as a foreigner, from the municipality of
Florence, an exemption from having soldiers
quartered in his house, an infliction which he
particularly dreaded. Relieved from this ap-
prehension, he shut himself up in his dwelling,
never venturing out, except for a walk of two

hours in the morning, which was essential to
his health, and for which he chose the most retired spots. But Alfieri had obtained too much
celebrity by his writings to be allowed to escape
individual observation: General Miollis, the
French commandant at Florence, had a taste
for literature, and was anxious to become acquainted with the greatest Italian dramatist. He
called several times on the Count, but the latter
was always invisible. Tired of these unavailing
visits, the General sent him a polite message,
requesting to know when he might be permitted to wait upon him. Alfieri returned a written answer, stating if the General, as commandant of Florence, ordered him to appear before
him, Vittorio Alfieri would obey him, as he never resisted the constituted authorities, what-
ever they might be ; but if he was actuated only
by individual curiosity, Alfieri, naturally unsoci-
able, wished to make no new acquaintance, and
requested the General to hold him excused.
The General immediately replied, that the
works of Alfieri had given him a great desire

to become acquainted with the author, but as that was disagreeable to him, he should not again importune him. This was the only annoyance Alfieri experienced during the two invasions of the French, from whom he expected little better than martyrdom; and the manner in which he conducted himself on this occasion reflects little credit on his urbanity and good sense.

The French General, however, was not singular in the repulse which he experienced from the haughty recluse. Alfieri, in his later years, studiously avoided the formation of new intimacies, and all letters addressed to him, unless directed by a well-known hand or under the seal of a friend, were usually thrown into the fire unopened. He never looked into the public journals or the periodical papers, and thus deprived himself of the means of learning the extent of that fame, which it had been the labour and object of his life to earn. He never appears to have suspected that he had obtained that high rank in the estimation of Italy and of

Europe which he deserved, and which he already possessed; and his wayward imagination rejected the only illusion which could cheer or irradiate his existence. The concluding years of his life were divided between a profound melancholy and a haughty irascibility. In his more tranquil intervals, he sometimes conversed with animation, but always with a degree of bitterness. At other times, he hardly ever spake in company, and as seldom smiled. His temper depended not a little on his favourite horse, which was led out to him every morning, and which he used to feed with his own hand. If the animal neighed, or exhibited any symptom of pleasure or gratitude, his countenance lost something of its austerity and gloom, but the insensibility of the horse to his caresses was usually accompanied by the increased dejection of the master. Alfieri passed a considerable portion of his time in the different churches, frequently sitting there, silent and motionless, from vespers to sunset, apparently absorbed in listening to the psalms of the monks, as they

1ose from behind the screen of the choir. His recorded opinions and the manner of his death would lead us to conjecture, that he did not seek these holy places to indulge in devout or penitent meditation, but to cherish a solemn and unearthly melancholy, and to mitigate the intensity of those turbulent feelings which harassed and maddened him.*

Piedmont, already revolutionized, had, in imitation of its French master, changed its *Royal Academy* of Sciences into a National Institute, on the plan of that of Paris, uniting the *belles lettres* with the fine arts. This society named

---

* His floating robe around him folding,
  Slow sweeps he through the column'd aisle ;
  With dread beheld, with gloom beholding
  The rites that sanctify the pile.
But when the anthem shakes the choir,
And kneel the monks, his steps retire ;
By yonder lone and wavering torch
His aspect glares within the porch ;
  There will he pause till all be done,
  And hear the prayer, but utter none.

          Byron's Giaour.

Alfieri a member of their Institute, and sent
him a letter, informing him of the appointment.
Alfieri, having been previously informed, by
Caluso, of their intention, returned their letter
unopened, and made known to them his rejec-
tion of the proffered honour in no very polite
terms. Their having addressed him by the title
of *citizen* was sufficient to rouse the dignified
resentment of the patrician bard. About this
time, Alfieri gave way to a new, or rather an
old impulse to write comedies, and arranged
the plots of six, out of twelve which he intended to compose. These pieces are much more
remarkable for their extravagance than for any
merit in the design or execution, and only excite our admiration of the persevering infatua-
tion of the author. One of them is a satire on
Italian marriages, and is entitled *The Divorce*.
The others are after the manner of Aristophanes,
and are all on political subjects. Three of
these, *L'Uno (The One) 1 Pochi (The Few)*
and *I Troppi (The Too Many)* expose the
faults of the monarchic, the aristocratic, and

the popular government; and a fourth teaches
us, that the One, the Few, and the Too Many,
should be blended together, and that their union
may compose a somewhat tolerable system. *Il
Finestrino* is a satire partly against religious im-
postors, but principally against the philoso-
phers, who would destroy the old religions
without substituting any other in their stead; a
bad one, in the opinion of the author, being
better than none at all. Anxious to develope
these heterogenous conceptions, which were intended to close his literary career, he resolved
to put forth all his remaining strength in their
composition. He wrote them in the same order
in which he had conceived them, and allotted
only six days for the developement of each.
This immoderate exertion brought on a severe
illness, before he had finished his fifth comedy.
His malady was violent and short, but was attended by a long convalescence; so that he was
not able to resume his labours until the latter
end of 1801. He then finished developing his
fifth and sixth comedies, and, having surmount-

ed this fatiguing task, he felt relieved from an insupportable burthen.

At the end of this year, he received intelligence of the death of his sister's only son, the young Count de Cumiana, in the flower of his age. - Though Alfieri had seen little of this youth, he was deeply afflicted at his death, and he felt some chagrin at seeing his possessions pass into the hands of strangers. His sister's three daughters were all married, and this event induced him to enter into new arrangements with her to secure the payment of his pension, that he might not be in any way dependent on his nieces or their husbands, with whom he was not at all acquainted. The peace of Amiens had restored some degree of tranquility in Italy; and the French having abolished the paper currency at Rome, as well as in Piedmont, Alfieri found himself delivered from the embarrassments he had experienced during the last five years. Estranged from the gaieties of life; plain in his attire, which was always black; seeing no company; and profuse only in the pur-

chase of books; he found himself amply rich
for a man of his unostentatious habits. In the
summer of 1802, he began versifying his comedies with the same ardour and application with
which he had conceived and developed them,
and again felt the evil effects of this unremitting
labour. Throughout these avocations, he never
infringed upon the three hours he had devoted
to reading and studying every morning. By the
time he had finished versifying two of his comedies, he was attacked by an inflammation in
the head : his body became covered with biles,
accompanied with an eresipelatous affection and
violent spasmodic pains, which confined him to
his bed for fifteen days. Caluso, who had promised him a visit in Tuscany for some years
past, arrived at this period, and remained with
him for twenty-seven days, the longest time that
his engagements at Turin would allow. The
Abbé read over to Alfieri his satires, his translations from the Greek, the Æneid and Terence,
with which he was well pleased. The comedies, Alfieri would not venture to show him,

considering them still too imperfect even for
the eye of friendship. On his departure, Alfieri sunk into a state of grief and despondency,
which it required all the care and attentions of
the Countess to alleviate. He was cured of his
disorder by the end of October, and immediately resuming his task, finished the versification of his comedies by the end of December.
Increasing infirmities reminded him of the resolution he had taken to close his literary career while in the full possession of his faculties.
He, however, continued to prosecute his studies, occasionally examining his own writings
for the purpose of correcting and polishing
them. He felt anxious to prepare an edition of
his unpublished works, but a dread of the harassing task of revision deterred him. He took
the precaution of leaving a correct manuscript
of those pieces which he thought worthy of seeing the light, and of burning the remainder.
Vain of having made himself master of the
Greek language at such an advanced period of
life, Alfieri hit upon a somewhat singular device

to reward and commemorate this exploit: this was the institution of THE ORDER OF HOMER, of which he enrolled himself a member. He caused a superb collar of THE ORDER to be made, of solid gold, richly ornamented with precious stones; and inscribed with the names of twenty-three poets, ancient and modern. To the collar was appended a cameo, with the head of Homer, and on the reverse two Greek verses of his own composition, and of which he made an Italian translation.* With the invention of this institution, which he flattered himself with the hope of perpetuating, Alfieri terminated his *Memoirs*, on the fourteenth of May, 1803. From this period, he relinquished all his literary pursuits, with the exception of his comedies, the completion of which was the principal object of his solicitude. The gout, which usually annoyed him in the changes of the seasons, attacked him in the spring of this year with unusual vio-

---

* Forse inventava Alfieri un Ordin vero
Nel farsi ei stesso Cavalier di Omero.

lence. His digestion had, for some years, been
difficult and painful: and, in order to ward off,
or, at least, to weaken the attacks of the gout,
he continued to diminish the quantity of food
which he allowed himself, moderate as it was,
convinced that a spare regimen was conducive
to his health and to his power of application.
In vain the Countess entreated him to abandon
a system of abstinence, under which his consti-
tution was evidently sinking: he continued obstinately to adhere to the resolution of starving
his disorder, and persisted in labouring on his
comedies, fearing that the approach of death
might deprive them of his finishing touches. He
also constantly devoted some hours every morning to reading, according to his custom for some
years, and in this manner continued to labour
and grow worse, until the latter end of autumn.
The presence and society of Caluso, who remained with him nearly the whole of this period,
assisted in dissipating the languor of this protracted illness. On the third of October, Alfieri
rose, apparently in better health and spirits than

usual ; and after his morning studies, went out
for an airing in his phaeton. He had scarcely
set out, when he was seized with a cold shiver-
ing : he alighted, expecting to dissipate it by
walking, but was attacked by an acute pain in
his bowels, which obliged him to return.   He
remained extremely ill with a fever during the
day, but was somewhat relieved in the evening.
He passed the night without much suffering,
though troubled with a continual inclination to
retch.   The next day he dressed himself, and
descended from his apartment to the hall to
dinner, but was unable to eat. He passed the
greater part of the day in sleep, and was extremely restless during the night. On the morning of the 5th, he wished to take the air, but was
prevented by the day being rainy. In the evening
he took his chocolate as usual, and with ap-
parent relish.   In the succeeding night the pain
in his bowels returned, and his physician ordered
sinapisms to be applied to his feet : they had
scarcely began to operate, when the Count
ordered them o be taken off, fearing that the

L

sores they produced would prevent his walking.
On the following morning the physician called
in another member of the faculty, and the result
of their consultation was to order fomentations
and blisters, to be applied to the lower extremi-
ties. To this remedy the patient, though evidently
in danger, obstinately refused to submit, as it
would deprive him of the use of his legs for
some time. He was visited in the course of the
day by a priest, whom he received with more
urbanity than was usual with him, but parried
the object of his visit by saying to him, " Have
the kindness to look in to-morrow': I trust that
death will wait for four-and-twenty hours." In
the evening he took a dose of opium, which
alleviated his pain, and procured him a tolerably
tranquil night. The relief thus obtained was
accompanied by occasional delirium: while this
lasted, he talked repeatedly of his studies, and
of his labours for thirty years, and repeated a
number of Greek verses from Hesiod, an author
whom he had never read but once. At six in
the morning the Countess, who had attended

him almost incessantly, retired to take some
repose. Contrary to the advice of his physicians,
Alfieri persisted in taking oil and magnesia,
which had speedily a prejudicial effect, and in
two hours he appeared in imminent danger.
The priest at this time made his appearance : he
found Alfieri sitting in his arm-chair, suffering
from a difficulty of breathing, which almost
choked him. " At present," said Alfieri, " I
imagine I have but a few minutes to spare," and
requested Caluso, who was present, to fetch the
Countess. When he saw her, he stretched out
his hand, exclaiming, " Clasp my hand, my
dear friend, I die." A moment after his eyes
became dim, and he expired.

Thus died Vittorio Alfieri, in his fifty-seventh
year, October the 8th, 1803. His remains were
deposited in the church of Santa Croce, at
Florence, near the tombs of Michael Angelo and
Machiavel, and a plain stone was laid over
them, till replaced by the splendid monument
which the Countess erected to his memory. It
is the work of Canova, but is considered as

being by no means one of his happiest conceptions. A little step, opposite the monument, is
shewn as the spot where the Countess periodi-
cally contemplates the tomb of her beloved
Alfieri.

THE END.

Maurice, Printer, Fencburch-street.

Printed in the United States
144755LV00006B/90/A

9 781104 146047